RESISTANCE TO CHANGE
A NEW PERSPECTIVE

By

Daniela Bradutanu, PhD

A Textbook for Managers
Who Plan to Implement a Change

RESISTANCE TO CHANGE

ISBN-13: 978-1517210090
ISBN-10: 1517210097

"The intention for this book is to present the resistance to change phenomenon from a new perspective. The term resistance is complex and very often misinterpreted. Change leaders should adapt their perspectives on this subject and try to see resistance from a positive angle as well. By just changing the prospect of analyzing it, managers could experience a greater success in implementing new changes and effectively attract more employees onto their side."

Daniela Bradutanu, PhD, Change Manager

Thank You

I would like to say thank you to my professors from the West University of Timişoara, Romania, especially to Mariana Predişcan, an amazing professor who believed in me and always challenged me. I would like to also thank Laurie W. Ford, an extraordinary person who gave me useful insights on change management. Also, I want to thank my extraordinary family. Thank you for your unconditional love and support.

Contents

Introduction

After completing a PhD in Management and seeing a need in the field, I decided to write this book. It took me three years to gather the necessary information and a few moments of insight to see the light at the end of the tunnel.

Through my studies in Romania I soon discovered that resistance to change was viewed by top managers only in one way – as a very negative phenomenon.

If employees thought that change was a bad thing, taking them out of their comfort zone, top managers, rather than analyzing their employees' reactions and trying to explain the benefits of the new implementations, viewed these individuals' resistance as an obstacle. In many cases the employees had no idea what was going to happen next and as people usually do they began to ask questions. Instead of answering their questions and involving employees in the process and trying to gain their trust and transforming them into "on board" members, some managers perceived their behavior as resistant. As some would say "Either you are obedient and do as you are told or you'll be fired."

Seeing how things were in my home country, I decided to expand my research territory beyond Romania and moved to New York. I discovered that the situation was totally different. After conducting more than 100 interviews and waiting patiently at several managers' doors, I soon realized that American managers actually welcomed the resistance from the employees' side, and that the employees were not afraid to manifest their personal opinions. On the contrary, I learned that if their idea was a good one, employees know they will be rewarded.

In light of these discoveries, my intention for this book is to present the resistance to change phenomenon from a new perspective. I have researched the phenomenon starting with the first published papers on the subject and resistance is mostly viewed as a negative thing. In Chapter I, I highlight the positive side of the concept by bringing solid arguments from experts in the Change Management field to support this idea. Their view is that resistance is not necessarily negative, and if used appropriately, change agents can actually gain from it.

It is generally accepted that people react differently to change, depending on their own assumptions. In order to reduce employees' resistance and gain their full cooperation, the change agent must first know what makes them opposed to this change. The main reasons why employees oppose change, as well as their determinants at both the individual and organizational level, are presented in Chapter II.

There are many forces that generate the appearance of the resistance to change phenomenon and they come from both inside as well as outside the company. After conducting extensive research, I have identified and classified these forces, proposing an original model of the forces that generate resistance to change within a company.

Since many managers do not always involve employees in the new processes or do not trust them enough to communicate important decisions, they are often confronted with a hostile behavior from their employees' perspective. In order to obtain employees' cooperation and support, I presented a few efficient methods to reduce their resistance in Chapter IV, by presenting methods that should be applied according to the identified reasons for the resistance to change.

Also by analyzing eleven organizational change models, I have found that the reducing resistance to change stage is present, absent, or inferred through the proposed reducing resistance to the change methods. As resistance is a complex phenomenon faced by many managers, in the last paragraph of Chapter V, I propose a model for reducing resistance to change which can be applied before, after or during the implementation stage of a change process, depending on the type of change.

CHAPTER 1

Resistance to Change - Today's Perspective

The term "resistance" used in the context of organizational change describes people's reluctance to give up the comfort of their status quo. Employees grow accustomed to a certain situation, form specific habits, and then find these habits very difficult to give up.

Resistance represents a natural reaction from people, regardless of the impact the change will have. The biggest problem is not the change itself, but management's inability to anticipate the employees' reluctance and to respond accordingly.

Can Resistance to Change be Misinterpreted?

Resistance to change is a well-known concept in the organizational change field, having been recognized for a long time as an important factor influencing the success of an organizational change effort. The resistance factor is considered by many managers and leaders as a real problem, as once manifested, it often leads to the failure of a change attempt. A study published by The Center for Creative Leadership reported that between 66% and 75% of all change initiatives fail—a depressing statistic for those trying to change an organization.[1] People

---

[1] Kee J.E., Newcomer Kathryn E. (2008), *Why Do Change Efforts Fail*, Public Manager, Potomac, Vol. 37, Issue 3, pp. 5-12.

entrusted to lead an organizational change process are often confronted with the experience of resistance to change, particularly resistance to change from the employees' side.

Most theories concerned with this change come from the management field which are often focused on a more efficient implementation of change, implementation that can be successful only if resistance to change from the employees' perspective is mitigated. This phenomenon is normally perceived as a negative thing that needs to be combated.

Many authors (Lawrence, 1954; Maurer, 1996; Strebel, 1996; Waddell and Sohal, 1998; and others) point out that the reasons for the failure of many change initiatives can be located in resistance to change. Indeed, in some cases this resistance represents a negative phenomenon which has adverse effects on organizational performance and therefore, must be overcome. This view was presented in the first published works on this topic, but over the years, after more debates on the subject, a positive side of the phenomenon was highlighted.

The term "resistance" is complex and very often misinterpreted. Change leaders should adapt their perspectives on this subject and try to see resistance from a positive angle as well. By just changing the prospect of analyzing it, managers could experience a greater success in implementing new changes and effectively attract more employees onto their side.

Furthermore, in order to answer the question of this resistance as a negative or a positive phenomenon, we will analyze two approaches identified in the literature. In "Reframing Resistance to Organizational Change" by Thomas Robyn and Cynthia Hardy, I have identified and outlined two distinct approaches to change resistance.

The most common approach in the literature is the **negative approach**, by which the change manager or agent has the right to use any means deemed necessary to effectively suppress resistance from the employees' side, considering that any opposition must be immediately alleviated. Although many organizations have adopted this approach for a long time, the success of change attempts was further reduced. In order to identify new ways to engage and involve staff in the process of organizational change, some researchers decided to expand the research field, proposing a **positive approach**. As Ford et al. (2008: 363) state "There are circumstances under which what agents call resistance can be a positive contribution to change."

From this new perspective, resistance is seen as a positive phenomenon with favorable effects on the change process. It is considered that the implementation of new organizational changes will be improved if the management will encourage expressions of resistance. Process improvement can be achieved through a dialogue between the resistant parties and the change agent, in which the change agent actually listens to what people are saying about how to implement a change – what specifics will or will not work.

In both cases, the change agent has the privilege of power. Whether employees exhibit resistance and the change agent has sufficient authority to apply coercive measures or whether being encouraged to manifest resistance in order to generate new ideas, employees do not provide ideas that are good enough to be considered. In both cases, employees are disadvantaged.

In order to highlight the positive side of resistance, I will emphasise three aspects that make this positive approach more effective.

1. Is resistance to change contrary to the interests of the organization?

In most cases, resistance is seen as contrary to the interests of the organization, undermining any change attempts. Although this statement is true in some cases, in others it is totally erroneous. Employees' resistance can also be a good thing, preventing the organization from making costly mistakes. Middle and lower level employees are those who perform routine tasks and often have sufficient knowledge to predict whether a particular change will be beneficial or not. Also, employees do not always put their personal interests in the foreground, being attentive to what happens with the organization. As long as the organization is powerful and prosperous, its members have a secure job. For this reason, employees will resist any change attempt that is considered to be harmful or threatening to the organization and their job security.

2. *Is resistance a negative behavior that involves controversy from the employees' side?*

While some employees may take legal and illegal actions, ethical and non-ethical, others lacking sufficient information may ask questions and get involved in discussions that highlight the negative aspects of the proposed changes [2]. Resistance can be interpreted as a response from the members involved in the process, who actually wish to express their views on the issues that affect them and are relevant to their personal security. Expression of anxiety and reluctance, as well as requesting more information, do not necessarily represent a manifestation of resistance or refusal to engage in the change process. Of course, each manager perceives resistance in his or her own way. For some, the request of too many answers equates with resistance. Instead of analyzing the overall situation and identifying the reasons that determine employees to be reluctant, such as doubt, lack of information, and the needed time to get used to the idea, managers classify these actions as defiant. A greater attention should be paid to the communication between managers and subordinates, as when the latter receive a clear explanation of what will happen, they will join the change process.

3. *Is resistance an intentional action?*

Resistance can occur on three levels: cognitive, affective, and behavioral. Very often, employees may perceive a new change as unnecessary and harmful and will express doubts about its success. They can experience emotions like anxiety, fear, frustration or even anger, either because the effects of previous changes have disadvantaged them or because in the past they did not perceive any gains from such

---

[2] Smollan R. (2011), Engaging with Resistance to Change, University of Ackland Business Review, Vol.13, No.1, p. 12..

experiences. Often an unconscious or semi-conscious sense of reluctance or refusal is manifested, which is interpreted as inertia. Employees' perceptions and feelings are recognized as resistant even when they do not always lead to negative behaviors. Although these perceptions and feelings may not trigger a direct resistance from the employees' side, they can have a corrosive effect on the employees' commitment to change. Instead of being excited to get involved in the change process, members of the organization can show a simple compliance or even indifference.

Through addressing these three questions we can conclude that resistance is not necessarily a negative phenomenon. As White (1998) states, "Change itself is neither good or bad, it is inevitable." This is true because resistance will certainly appear, regardless of its type, in one way or another and it will affect the people involved. Since many employees perceive a new change as an uncertainty regarding their future, most likely they will associate it with a loss. Resistance to change, however, can be seen as a positive phenomenon as well. Depending on the situation and how the people in charge of implementing a new change perceive the employees' actions, resistance can be either a positive or a negative phenomenon.

One of the biggest mistakes that change leaders make is to assume that resistance has no merit. Individuals who manifest resistance can provide valuable insights on how the proposed change can be modified in order to increase its chances of success (Michelman, 2007: 3).

This resistance is a natural phenomenon, representing an energy that needs to be corectly channeled in order to obtain superior results. It offers a degree of stability and the knowledge of how employees will react to a change follows a predictable organizational behavior. In this way, the chaotic mess is avoided and debates among employees are stimulated. By manifesting resistance and challenging debates between employees and managers, the organizational change process can be significantly improved, as new ideas can be identified. As a result of such debates, issues that were not previously considered can be taken into account or can be improved, thanks to the flow of new ideas.

The main objectives of any organization are to refine its performance and to improve or find new ways to more efficiently use its resources and capacities. To achieve these objectives faster and cheaper, it is recommended for change agents to take into account the views of the members involved in the process. Often employees from middle and lower levels may see certain aspects invisible to the organization's management. Because of this response, some companies encourage their employees' resistance. It is considered that it will both enhance the communication between organizational levels and have positive effects on the future development of the organization.

Resistance to Change - A Potential Asset

Many authors do not consider employees' resistance as a potential asset that contributes to a more efficient implementation or a positive phenomenon, nor do they consider that resistance can generate creative ideas. Instead these ideas favor the change agents, justifying their actions to label as resistant even the positive contributions that employees provide. Therefore, most of the reviewed literature recognizes only the negative approach of resistance to change, an approach that very often is incorrect.

"By assuming that resistance is necessarily bad, change agents have missed its potential contributions of increasing the likelihood of successful implementation, helping build awareness and momentum for change, and eliminating unnecessary, impractical, or counterproductive elements in the design or conduct of the change process (Ford et al., 2008: 363)." The change agent, therefore, must not dispose of the entire resistance expressed within the organization. Some of it might be valuable and not always the most disgruntled employees are the most defiant. Not always are employees' reactions towards a change considered obstacles, as they might represent resources as well and contribute to a better implementation of the change process. By communicating publicly the decision of implementing a new change and through debating the subject with the employees, change agents can identify important aspects that as of yet have not been found.

Instead of trying to eliminate or suppress employees' resistance, managers should rather use their reactions in a positive framework. Resistance may be useful as feedback and therefore, managers can use it to improve and refine the organizational change process.

Furthermore, three situations that highlight the positive aspects of resistance to change are presented here, supporting the argument that resistance can also represent a potential resource.

> ➤ *Opposing resistance and discussing the issues between employees helps to spread the change decision.* To attract employees onto their side, change agents must constantly communicate with them. Of course, the new ideas will be more slowly accepted and the change agent must make a greater effort to notify all the affected people of the changes that will take place in the organization. For the subject of the new change to become widely known, resistance's manifestation is more than welcome. In fact, the goal is that the employees debate the subject among themselves and get actively involved in discussions. Whether the talks are positive or negative, the essential thing is to catch the employees' attention. As Czarniawska and Sevon (1996) stated, "if people want a change to die, they would be better off not talking about it than engaging in existence-giving "resistance" communications that provide energy and further its translation and diffusion." On the contrary, employees get actively involved in discussions, generating the necessary energy to spread the change initiatives. For this reason, the emergence of resistance can be beneficial.

> ➤ *Resistance can be used to engage people in a change process through paradoxical interventions* (Torma and Petty, 2004). This method of getting employees to do exactly what is desired is characterized by prohibiting their involvement in achieving the desired work. They will resist instructions and without noticing, will head towards the targeted objective.

11

> ➤ *Resistance may be useful as feedback* (Ford and Ford, 2010: 369). Managers who believe that resistance to change from the employees' side represents the main cause that determines the failure of an organizational change process lose an important leverage in implementing a change. Resistance represents feedback and when seen as feedback, it can help improve the change process. Taking into account the employees' comments and criticisms, the change agent can adjust certain aspects and in such a way improve the change process. Although most managers perceive signs of resistance as adverse effects, they should consider their absence as signs of alarm. A reckless acceptance of any change decision may have unfavorable effects in the future, inasmuch as employees in the end will usually accept all decisions.

The Value of Resistance to Change

Over the past decades, resistance to change has been recognized as a critical factor that leaves either a positive or a negative imprint on change processes.

More than half of the organizational changes that were attempted to be implemented in organizations failed and according to the opinions of the involved managers, the main reason is the resistance to change. For all that, viewed from another perspective, resistance can represent a valuable resource in implementing a new change. What, then, is the value of resistance?

The value of resistance has been highlighted since the '60s, when researchers found that managers can "learn" from it. Therefore, the phenomenon cannot be ignored. These results contradicted the theories of classical management, according to which resistance represents an obstacle in the way of change that must be overcome or removed. Because of such assumptions, for a long period, resistance has been perceived as an undesirable and harmful phenomenon that generated only conflicts within an organization.

According to the authors Jeffrey D. Ford and Laurie W. Ford (2010: 24), change leaders should stop blaming resistance and start using it more effectively. Three aspects have been identified by the above-mentioned authors, who highlight why resistance to change should be used when implementing a change.

➤ *Blaming resistance can be dysfunctional for managers who perceive resistance as a threat*

Managers who perceive resistance from their subordinates' side as purely a negative and threatening phenomenon can become competitive and non-communicative and be more concerned about winning and looking good in front of others, than implementing the change. In order to maintain their authority and be more focused on themselves than on the entire change process, these managers can categorize subordinates as obstacles and dispose of potential change partners, who could in fact represent assets.

Each manager interprets resistance in his own way. If a certain employee's behavior can be classified as negative by some managers, others may perceive the same behavior as positive. An example is in the communication of the change decision. Depending on the interpretation of the resistance to change phenomenon, for some change agents, asking too many questions is associated with a negative behavior, while for others, the absence of questions indicates a total lack of interest. Thus, two opposite behaviors may be perceived as resistant.

Responding in a negative way to the behaviors perceived as resistant may be damaging for managers; they voluntarily are ignoring the opportunities to improve and refine the change process and thus are losing the confidence of valuable employees. So far, the failure of many organizational change processes can be attributed to the managements' inability to perceive the positive aspects of resistance.

➤ *Resistance is a bilateral phenomenon*

It is incorrect to state that resistance is located just "there, in them", referring only to the employees involved in the change process.

Considering that only the affected employees can resist change, the possibility that the change agent can be resistant to employees' ideas and proposals is ignored. We can affirm that resistance to change from the employees' side is at least partially dependent on the change leader's behavior. For a productive implementation of a change process, both sides need to be considered.

> ➤ *Blaming resistance is incomplete, because it ignores its value*

Managers who consider this resistance as a negative and dysfunctional phenomenon assume that it represents an obstacle in the way of progress, increases the amount of work required to be fulfilled, and only serves the personal interests of those who manifest it. Depending on the situation, resistance can represent both an asset and a liability. In order to achieve a greater flexibility in the organizational change field and to reduce this opposition more efficiently, I recommend a more general approach to the phenomenon.

"We can label as resistance virtually every type of behavior, ranging from a roll of the eyes to overt sabotage."[3] Usually, managers consider those behaviors and discussions as resistant that they either do not like or those that involve extra work on their part.

People usually ask many questions because they are curious about the changes that will take place in the organization and it is absurd to assume that all members of the organization intentionally manifest resistance.

Of course, based on their own perceptions of the change process, the employees' interests may be polar opposite from the managers' interests. However, before classifying the employees' behavior as defiant, the change agent should respond to at least two questions:

1. Why do we call such reaction from the employees' side resistance?

2. If we would consider resistance as feedback, how could it help improve the change process?

---

[3] Ford J. D., Ford Laurie W. (2010), *Stop Blaming Resistance to Change and Start Using It*, Organizational Dynamics, Vol. 39, No. 1, pp. 24.

Answering these two questions, the change agent could change his perspective on the resistance to change phenomenon and modify his behavior in order to more easily attract the employees to his side.

Why is Resistance to Change Blamed?

The tendency to blame resistance in the case of an organizational change process failure is due to three forces, namely: preconceived opinions, social dynamics, and management errors (Ford and Ford, 2010: 25).

1. Preconceived opinions

According to the opinions of psychologists, people often make mistakes when trying to explain the successes and failures they were part of. In most cases, a project's success and positive effects are attributed to the manager/ change agent's efforts, abilities and involvement. On the other hand, when a project fails, the manager/ change agent does not attribute any blame to himself but to the other members involved, the external factors or even bad luck. Therefore, success is usually associated with the change agent's capabilities and talents, while failure is mainly due to financial and human resources.

Research on performance evaluation found that managers tend to blame their subordinates when a poor organizational performance is recorded, while the latter blame external factors, often mentioning the lack of support from the managers' side. Therefore managers who encounter difficulties during a change process are likely to assign the impediments to the employees' resistance and to the effects of the external factors.

2. Social Dynamics

No manager likes to encounter difficulties or even fail at implementing a new project, as inevitably, this might attract a decrease of confidence from the employees' side or even loss of status. The change agents are considered professionals from whose part success is expected. Any mistake made in the current business environment, characterized by an increased competitiveness, can contribute to the change agent's loss of authority or even his job. Because of this, when difficulties are encountered, the change agents must communicate to the employees what is happening in the organization and how they plan to overcome the obstacles encountered. Of course, in order to not create agitation among employees and to maintain their degree of confidence, the change agents will have to minimalize the difficulties they are faced with, and which undoubtedly are considered belonging to employees. Blaming resistance is a socially accepted explanation among managers, because „everyone" knows that people resist change. Thus, in order to protect their image, managers usually transfer any difficulties they encounter to the employee(s).

3. Management Errors

During an organizational change process it is inevitable for a change agent not to commit at least one mistake. Although many commit mistakes, only a few are able to recognize them. Four mistakes are the most common, these being:

1. The interruption or termination of communication with employees and failure to restore their confidence

Establishing agreements of understanding between change agents and employees, as well as gaining the trust of their employees is essential if an efficient implementation is desired. Breakdown in communication, regardless of its nature, may create mistrust and reluctance from the employees with respect to future change attempts. Any promise made must be respected, otherwise, the manager's credibility will be affected.

A common mistake frequently encountered in large organizations with adverse effects on the financial performance and organizational culture is missing a deadline and failure of the budgetary targets. In terms of organizational culture, the negative effects are found in loss of credibility. According to a study by American researchers, 64% of employees do not trust their superiors. Over the years, these negative effects become rooted in the organization's culture.

2. *The tendency to present with an excessive and unjustified enthusiasm the benefits of change and minimize its negative effects*

In order to attract more employees on their side, many managers tend to make this mistake. They emphasize in an apathetic way the positive aspects of the process, totally or partially ignoring the negative aspects. Problems arise when these employees find out that they have been deceived. They lose respect and trust in the company's management, causing them to become more cautious regarding future change decisions. Typical reactions include requesting more explanations and challenging certain decisions. This behavior, which implies avoiding future possible misinterpretations of the employees, is often perceived as opposition by managers.

3. *Manifestation of uncertainty from the manager's side towards the change process*

When a change decision is communicated, the manager must be very explicit. He is the change agent, the person who inspires, motivates and attracts employees to the change's side. The manager may communicate to subordinates that certain objectives must be met during the year, but from previous experiences he/she knows they won't be met in time, and therefore, through his/her behavior, the agent misleads employees. When a manager fails to properly communicate the necessary information in order to obtain the employee's support to fulfill a certain goal, his credibility is compromised. Giving evidence of ambivalence in the statements made, employees tend to choose the most convenient solution for themselves. Why should they fulfill an objective on time when they know from past experience, its term may be extended?

4. *Unethical behavior*

In order to achieve success and enjoy the support of the organization's employees, the change agent must show honesty and integrity. Any violation of the practices, principles or values might lead to the ethical discreditation of the manager's authority, which involves jeopardizing the employees' commitment. The employees' behavior can be considered resistant, as they will no longer manifest constant support and will be more reluctant to the change process.

Reasons and Signs of Opposition

Reasons of Opposition

For most managers involved in an organizational change process, resistance to change from the employees' side represents a real challenge as it represents a phenomenon that occurs when employees do not support the change efforts. This is due to several reasons. If the classical theories were more concerned about how to overcome this resistance, the phenomenon being considered a negative one, then the concepts of the modern theory are based on another axiomatic principle. The aim of these theories is the attempt to explain and understand the emergence of the resistance phenomenon, taking more interest in its causes than the ways in which it can be overcome.

The ultimate goal is to implement a new change with minimum opposition, focusing on preventing the phenomenon's appearance rather than defeating an already expressed resistance. Thus, for a successful implementation, the change agent first must identify the main reasons that generate employees' resistance and only after this work has been done, can the agent proceed to overcome it.

Before presenting the main reasons that cause the appearance of the resistance to change phenomenon, I would like to specify that resistance can occur at three levels, namely: individual, group and organizational levels. I've classified the identified reasons into two categories, respectively: *reasons at the individual and group level and reasons at the organizational level.*

Reasons at the individual and group level

Resistance to change is not surprising, therefore it needs to be regarded as a normal reaction as "most people are afraid of the revolutionary way life can change, and also, have their own views on how to implement a change." Individuals and groups subject to a change are faced with the fact that the communication channels, both formal and informal, as well as the behavioral patterns are different. Consequently, they will easily respond to calls to resistance, representing a strong deterrent.

As a result of change, people can perceive such feelings as accomplishment, loss, pride or stress. "On the other hand, a change process can generate uncertainty, ambiguity, loss of control and predictability (Muchinsky, 2000)." Marquis and Huston (2009: 176) argue that "because change disrupts the homeostasis or balance of the group, resistance should always be expected."

Changes in organizations are always accompanied by friction and as Harvey (1995) stated, "change without resistance is no change at all – it is an illusion of change." Although the emergence of resistance is inevitable, as stated in the previous chapter, this phenomenon is not necessarily a negative one. Representing a normal reaction from employees, it can be seen as feedback. For this reason, an effective manager will not try to avoid the phenomenon, on the contrary, he will try to understand and use it more effectively in implementing the new changes. Understanding the reasons behind the change can help managers or change agents to implement more effectively a change. Indeed, once the reasons are identified, the change agents would be able to more easily develop change management strategies, as well as find the best ways to reduce the resistance.

The idea according to which "people resist change" has recently been subject to criticism. Dent and Goldberg (1999) argue that people do not resist change itself, but rather the potential effects and negative consequences associated with it such as loss of status, loss of pay or loss of comfort. It's obvious that the organization's members will oppose any change attempts perceived as threatening or that might have negative repercussions on them. Nobody wants to do extra work for the same pay or be demoted because he or she does not hold sufficient knowledge to operate the new information system.

Manifestation of this opposition represents an attempt to preserve the traditions, norms and principles which the opposing parties deem valuable. In some cases, resistance can be described as a struggle for the control of the situation, between those who want to implement a change and those who prefer to maintain the status quo. The system tries to retain its unique character and therefore, the opposing parties act as an agent that protects its stability. The sudden implementation of many changes can lead to conflicts of interest between managers and subordinates. An example is that although promoting an employee on a higher position is considered to be a positive change, it can be perceived as a negative one if the person prefers stability at the expense of new opportunities and challenges.

In my opinion, managers should cautiously approach different reactions towards change. The origins of an employee's opposition may be at an individual, group and organizational level. It is important to investigate the extent to which resistance is directly related to the change. Perhaps this is simply a way of expressing other conflicts and tensions. I recommend assessing the situation globally, taking all factors into account.

To overcome resistance to change we need to answer at least two questions:

- What are the factors that lead individuals to manifest resistance?

- And how can we act on these factors to eliminate or substantially reduce them?

I will answer the first question here and the second question will be answered in Chapter IV.

Researching the literature, I have found that in some instances, certain employees exhibit a stronger opposition compared to others. In the following table I have categorized six reasons to this change that exert a great influence on the employees' behavior, both at the individual and the group level. I have also listed the determinants.

Reasons and determinants of resistance to change

No.	Reasons	Determinants
1.	Personal interest	- Job security - Personal gain - inadequate remuneration - Maintaining social relationships
2.	Misunderstanding of the new change's objectives and strategies	- The goal of change is not clearly defined - Inadequate information - Lack of involvement of the affected employees in the planning phase - The affected employees do not realize the need for change
3.	Loss of control	- Alterations in the daily activity - Fear of the unknown - Fear of incompetence (lack of the necessary knowledge to execute the new tasks)
4.	Different estimations regarding the intended change	- Distinct perception of the change plans - Low credibility of the change agent
5.	Low tolerance towards change	- Unpleasant experiences in the past - Too high intellectual and/or emotional costs - Lack of personal confidence
6.	The effect of surprise	- The disparity between the new change and organizational culture - Performing additional activities

1. How does personal interest affect resistance to change?

The organizational change process may be perceived as a loss of personal benefits. If employees foresee potential personal damages as a result of a new change implementation, opposition is guaranteed. What person will decide to cooperate and contribute to the implementation of something that will not bring anything in return, and on the contrary, may even cause some losses?

The fear of personal loss is one of the biggest barriers to change faced by various organizations (Daft, 2000; Griffin, 2008). This is largely due to human nature as employees' see their personal interests as more important than those of the organization. Such a natural and universal behaviour is not actually dangerous, but its development can lead to the formation of some informal groups whose policies may aim to slow down the proposed changes.

Personal interest is characterized by the desire to not lose something valuable and employees putting an important emphasis on stability. This stability is ensured by *employment security, maintaining the personal gain* and *social relations.* Threatening such losses due to the implementation of a new change will lead to strong opposition from employees. Job loss will jeopardize the very existence of the individual and his family. A reduced income or more responsibilities will negatively affect the employee's interests, since the employee undoubtedly has some investments planned for the coming years based on the current salary or even other activities after work. Also, while working together for a period of time, colleagues establish certain relationships which when suddenly interrupted may create a state of frustration and discomfort. From these perceptions, the employees' personal interests represent a very important reason why they will resist and the change agent must pay attention to maintaining its stability.

2. Why is there a perceieved misunderstanding of the new change's objectives and strategies?

The misunderstanding of the new change's objectives and strategies usually occurs because employees are not able to assess the impact of the new change. As a result *of the lack of relevant information* regarding the objectives and modalities of implementing the change, and *the unclear definition of its purposes*, employees can form their own opinions, sometimes erroneous ones. In order to gain employees' support, the change agent must *involve them in the process starting with the planning stage*. This is necessary; otherwise employees may not *realize the need for change.*

3. Why is there loss of control?

Loss of control represents a strong reason why employees' oppose new changes, especially for those who hold management positions or have a certain seniority in the organization. Employees are afraid that associated with the new implementations *the work characteristics will be altered* and they will not be knowledgeable enough to cope with the new changes. To avoid being demoted, resistance's manifestation represents the ideal solution. Since most change initiatives are associated with uncertainty, *the fear of incompetence* and *the unknown* causes employees to become reluctant to everything new. They feel confused about the new activities that they will have to perform and managers are also confused about how to assess their subordinates' performances. As stated by Năstase (2009: 81), "employees must understand that in order to cope with change, they must manage learning." The role of top management is to intervene with as many training offers as possible so that employees feel they are able to carry on the new situation which will also help reduce their resistance.

4. What are some different estimations regarding the intended change?

The different estimates of the intended change are directly related to the *distinct perception of the change plans and objectives.* Managers and employees can perceive the value of change differently. Often, in an unjustified way, those who propose to implement a new change assume that employees perceive the benefits of the new implementation in the same way they do, and that everyone holds relevant information about the positive modifications that will occur. This belief is wrong, especially in those cases where *the degree of confidence in the change agent's actions is low* and where there are multiple sources of information. In such situations, it is advisable to choose either a change agent from within the organization who enjoys the respect and trust of his colleagues, or to bring in a consultant or a team of consultants outside the company. Effective communication between the change agent and the affected members is essential.

5. Why is there a low tolerance towards change?

Some people have a low tolerance for any change out of the fear that they will not be able to adapt to the new work requirements. They *do not have self-confidence.* It is human nature to be affected by life experiences such as the positive or negative impact of previous changes. People who have experienced unnecessary changes or changes that caused them damage or hurt, tend to be very suspicious regarding any change attempts. Thus, employees who in the past have gone through *unpleasant experiences* with respect to the changes that have been implemented or who have been caused serious *intellectual and/ or emotional effects,* that were way too high compared to the received benefits, will show a stronger reluctance.

6. How is the effect of surprise manifested?

Often, a change decision is made quickly and employees are taken by surprise. Not being prepared or informed about what is going to happen, they have no alternative but to show opposition, at least until they find out more information. Working in a company for a certain period of time, employees become familiar with its culture and *any disparity between the new change and the organizational culture* represents an unpleasant surprise which will lead to their contention. Also, the need to *perform additional activities* as a result of someone's dismissal is considered an unpleasant surprise since employees do not expect to take over another colleague's tasks. Unfortunately, this aspect is frequently encountered as employees are overloaded and have to multitask.

The reasons employees manifest resistance vary from one situation to another, depending on the personnel's ability to adapt to new changes.

A hardly surprising thing is that those who most need a change are those who are often against it (Năstase, 2009: 82). This concerns employees, managers, groups and the entire organization. In order to reduce resistance more effectively, I suggest first detecting the determinants and subsequently, eliminating them one by one.

Reasons at organizational level

The main reasons that generate resistance to change from the organization's side include the following elements:

1. **A high degree of bureaucracy** – This is characterized by a large number of regulations, rules and procedures within the organization; regulations that the more there are, the more restrictive they become, representing impediments in the way of implementing a new change. Changing one regulation inevitably will leave its mark on the others since they are all interconnected.

2. **The organizational culture** – This is represented as a powerful resistance to the change factor as it contains the values, norms and habits that form the organization. The core element of an adaptive change is that employees' actions should be aligned with their thoughts and feelings (Moore, 2011: 16). It is very difficult, if not impossible, to effectively implement a change that does not comply with the organization's values and norms.

3. **Group inertia** – This factor represents one of the personnel's reactions when faced with the change decision. Over time, employees get used to certain rules and procedures, form certain habits and establish particular friendships. When announced, the change decision is perceived as a threat that comes to destabilize things that were stable up to that point. The group inertia acts as a counter balance designed to ensure the organization's stability. Also, individuals will always comply with the rules of the group they belong to. If the group's leadership opposes the new change, its members will inevitably oppose it too.

4. **The reduced involvement of managers** – This element will represent a powerful factor of reluctance to change manifested from the organization's side or some of its departments. Managers need to communicate with their staff members at each stage of the process and try to involve them as much as possible. The middle and bottom managers are the main actors who interact with their subordinates, holding the necessary key levers to stimulate them to be part of the change process and contribute to its better implementation.

5. **Insufficient resources** – When a new change is scheduled, the presence of the necessary resources is vital for successful implementation. A change requires the resources of capital, time, and people with different abilities, but those that pose the biggest problems usually have a financial nature. Each new implementation has a budget, and failure to comply with it will surely have adverse effects. One example is an organization that decides to purchase a more performant informational program, but if the management will not have sufficient financial resources to send its employees to trainings to learn how to use it, the change will be in vain. There must be sufficient financial resources to fund all activities, people able to perform certain functions, as well as the necessary technologies. The lack of these resources can lead to a conflict within the organization. Another important aspect is that the limited resources can affect not only the organizations with insufficient incomes, but also the wealthier ones. The latter may encounter difficulties due to some investments that cannot be easily written off. It is recommended that managers and change agents pay particular attention to this issue otherwise, the entire change process may fail.

Forms and Signs of Opposition

Following a study by Sheffield University it was found that in each organizational change process, employees will be divided into three categories:

- Those who accept change (about 20%)

- Those who resist change (about 30%)

- Those who are waiting, without getting involved (about 50%)

Analyzing the above categories, we can conclude that half of the members of an organization do not have a personal opinion regarding the new change and often are undecided. Since employees who show resistance represent only 30%, it is recommended for the change agent to act and try to obtain the compliance of the undecided employees. They represent the majority and at the same time are the most vulnerable group. The change agent must convince them of the need for change, present the future benefits and involve them as quickly as possible in the process. Attracting a large percentage of the undecided employees can help ensure successful implementation of the new change.

According to Christopher W. Musslewhite and Robyn D. Ingram from the *The Center for Creative Leadership* from Greensboro, N.C., each person has a preference for how to embrace change. About a quarter of the population prefers a change to be entered slowly and gradually. Another quarter prefers radical changes. The remaining half however, prefers that the changes are pragmatic, practical and realistic.

According to this typology, employees' resistance to change is manifested in different forms. The most common are *direct, implicit, immediate, or deferred resistance.* The direct and immediate resistance are more easily identified, as they assume a direct opposition to any change attempt, complaints from employees, as well as a slowdown in activity. *The implicit* and *deferred resistance* are more difficult to recognize, in some cases representing a real challenge for managers. These two forms are manifested more subtly than the first two, being characterized by a loss of loyalty towards the organization, a reduced motivation to work or even loss of it, an increased absenteeism due to "health problems", increasing errors, as well as delayed actions necessary for implementing the change. From the organization's management point of view, the first two forms of resistance are preferred because they are easier to spot and managers can deal with them better than the other two.

Depending on the potential losses associated with the change processes, each employee will express his disagreement. Of course, each will perceive the new change in his own way.

The most common ways of expressing disagreement towards a change have been identified as:

- Denial of the need for change

- Indifference

- Indirect resistance - demonstrating their own incompetence

- Postponing actions necessary for achieving the change

- Impatient behavior

- Undue caution

Researching the literature, I have found that the most common way of expressing disagreement with a change is *its denial.* Employees deny any change idea arguing that it is not necessary either because they don't grasp certain problems or because they simply do not wish to see them. Since any change is associated with a potential loss, such reaction is considered normal. The management must not ignore such a response, on the contrary, they should pay attention, communicating to the employees the problematic situation the organization is facing and presenting their solutions. If the management, for example, will not get involved, such action, actually nonaction from their side, might lead to a future increase of employee resistance with the possibility that any change attempt will be met with a refusal.

Often, employees do not express opinions either for or against new implementations, but rather are simply *indifferent.* Such behavior, characterized by a lack of interest towards a change can have negative effects on their activity. Being distrustful of the success of the new change and starting from the preconception that its chances of success are minimal, members might not engage in the organizational change process. They will not learn the new aspects of their work, following that when the new project fails, they will only confirm their initial hypothesis: the change did not deserve any special attention from their side.

Opposition to change can also occur indirectly by demonstrating *incompetence*. Wishing to maintain the old routines and determined to show their disagreement with the new change implementation, employees may perform some tasks according to the old procedures or commit intentional errors.

For personal reasons, through loss of status and/ or authority within the organization, some employees may manifest resistance by *delaying actions necessary for implementing the new change.* If members feel they are not involved in the process and realize that some information is hidden, they can intentionally obstruct the new implementation, delay its progress or even sabotage the whole process.

Another aspect that could lead to the failure of an organizational change process is *employee impatience.* They get involved in the process but being eager to see prompt results, after a short period of time during which they did not perceive any benefits, conclude that the process was a total failure. Not being confident in the success of the implementation from the start by getting involved, they only confirm its uselessness. Expressing disagreement towards a change by adopting an impatient behavior can be very misleading for change agents. If initially they think that employees understand the need for change and agree to engage in the process, subsequently change agents discover that employees have never been confident in its success and were involved only for public facade. Lacking quick gains, however small they might be, or because of the lack of communication of their existence from the manager's side, employees' resistance can increase.

Undue caution is another way of expressing disagreement with change. When not having sufficient information about the new change, employees would rather oppose it than discover later that their interests have been harmed. Although sometimes employees are aware of the need of a new change, they prefer to be cautious. Foreseeing potential losses of benefits and even a possible failure of the change process, they will oppose any attempt that might destabilize their status quo.

Forces that Generate Resistance to Change within an Organization

A Model of the Forces that Generate Resistance to Change

For a long time employees were considered the only force generating resistance to change within an organization. But, with the expansion of research studies, experts in the field have identified other forces. In addition to the company's employees, Prediscan (2004: 132) has identified four forces related to the organizational climate: communications, organizational structure, management style and organizational culture.

By analyzing the literature, I have found that there may be other forces generating opposition to change, some from within the company, while others outside it.

In Figure 1 I have presented an original model of the forces that generate resistance to change and as it can be seen, the model is composed from three categories of forces. The first category is represented by the members involved in an organizational change process, which are the employees and stakeholders, and the change agent. The second category refers to the organizational environment, which generate the following change elements: organizational culture, organizational structure, management style, personnel policy, and the information system. The third category is represented by the economic environment, an external force for the organization but which has a considerable influence on it.

Figure 1: A model of the forces that generate resistance to change

Unlike the elements identified in the literature, in the category of the members who oppose change I've included the employees, the stakeholders and the change agent. The change agents can generate resistance as well, either through their actions or by the way they interpret the behavior of the affected staff.

In the second category, entitled "organizational environment", I have presented five forces which include culture, organizational structure, management style, personnel policy, and the information system. In addition to the evidence submitted by Prediscan (2004), I considered it was imperative to introduce in the model the personnel policy, too, as it plays an important role in attracting employees on the management's side, thus, obtaining their support for a smooth change implementation.

And last but not least, I found it necessary to add another force, this time external to the organization but which largely influences the behavior of the staff. The economic environment is a very important force generating resistance to change within an organization, whereas depending on the national economic situation, employees will exhibit a lower or a higher degree of resistance. Most organizations adapt their activities according to the economic environment. If the economy is growing, organizations can expand their activities, more jobs become available, and respectively, there are more opportunities for employees. On the other end of the spectrum, there are the situations when the economy is in recession, registering negative values. In such cases, employees' resistance to change will be much reduced or even non-existent, as they try by all means to keep their jobs and show support towards the management's decisions. To better understand these different forces, I will present a more detailed presentation of each of them.

Description of the Model's Components

I. Members involved in the organizational change process

Employees and Stakeholders

Any act of resistance to change is attributed to "the employees"; those persons who meet the management's decisions with a refusal of involvement or acceptance.

Although often it is considered that only employees from lower levels can manifest resistance, studies show that the middle and upper level managers, as well as other stakeholders can also express resistance. It is expected that higher level managers who have worked for a long time in the same company will oppose vehemently any change initiatives that could affect their positions or status. Of course, being forced to maintain the company's competitiveness on the market, they will implement new changes but they will rather be incremental and low-risk than radical and with a high level of uncertainty.

Employees from all organizational levels will oppose less favorable working conditions characterized by additional work and lower wages, a reduced status in the organization, or even loss of employment. In times of crisis or when a restructuring is being conducted, all stakeholders expect certain losses. Employees foresee the possibility of being fired or losing certain benefits, customers predict the possibility of higher prices, contracts with certain suppliers may cease as a result of less activities or modification of the used technology, and the state projects a reduction in the taxes to be collected.

It is considered logical that under such circumstances the organization's members and stakeholders will oppose the new change. Although it is often stated that regardless of the nature of the change, be it good or bad, employees will oppose the change, I found that this is not always true.

Research in organizational justice shows that employees react differently to any change attempt, depending on how they believe they are treated by management. If they ascertain that they are treated fairly, employees will develop attitudes and behaviors associated with successful change even in conditions of possible losses.[4] Contrary to this are the situations where employees feel they are misled, manipulated, or even treated unjustly. Their behavior will suddenly become negative, being characterized by decrease in productivity, an increase in thefts, a lack of cooperation and a diminished confidence in the change agent. Of course, each employee will react differently, depending on the impact he believes the change will have on him. From the employees' point of view such behavior is justified, representing a response to the injustices that have resulted.

According to Caruth et al. (1985), Kotter and Schlesinger (1979) and O'Toole (1995), many of the answers to this injustice were qualified as resistance, suggesting that resistance can be the result of the perceived injustices and misunderstandings between the change agent

---

[4] Cobb A. T., Wooten K. C., Folger R. (1995), *Justice in the Making: Toward Understanding the Theory and Practice of Justice in Organizational Change and Development,* Research in Organizational Change and Development, pp. 243-295.

and the organization's members. The violation of the existing rules and procedures as a result of the new change implementation can lead to the erosion of employees' trust and loss of credibility of the change agent. However, if the change agent presents a clear and formal justification on what happened, admits his guilt and asks employees' help, confidence can be restored and resistance reduced.

In 1969, through the article "How to deal with resistance to change", Paul Lawrence for the first time made the distinction between the resistance generated by technical aspects and the resistance generated by social ones. To highlight the differences, the author offered two examples of change in the used technology. In the first case, the structure of the social relationships between employees was not affected and as a result the manifestation of resistance was very low, almost nonexistent. In the second case, when a new assembly line was introduced, the degree of resistance to change was very high. The author's conclusion was that resistance to change is directly proportional to the degree to which the set of social relations of the organization is affected.[5] This statement is valid for all levels of the organizational pyramid.

I think that it is wrong to assert that employees oppose all change initiatives. Following the interviews with employees of a credit institution from Romania and the conducted study, I found that many employees welcome the new change initiatives.[6] As a result of a change, many employees foresee some personal gains and an increase in the organization's efficiency, both with positive effects on them.

Finally, it should be recognized that the members of an organization can easily accept certain aspects of a change and reject others. Therefore, the manager or the change agent should analyze the overall situation, taking into account all of the factors outlined above.

---

[5] Lawrence P. (1969), *How to Deal with Resistance to Change*, Harvard Business Review, vol. 32, no. 3, pp. 49-57.

[6] Bradutanu Daniela (2012), *DO REALLY EMPLOYEES RESIST CHANGE? CASE STUDY AT A CREDIT INSTITUTION*, Proceedings of the International Conference **Challenges of the Knowledge Society,** "Pro Universitaria" edition, Bucharest, pp. 1263-1268.

The Change Agent

By assuming that only employees can manifest resistance, the possibility that change agents can manifest it as well is being ignored. But before proceeding further, I consider it necessary to first define the term *change agent*.

The American Heritage Dictionary defines the *change agent as* "a person who gives expert or professional advice." Ford et al. (2008: 362) state that the *change agent* refers "to those who are responsible for identifying the need for change, creating a vision and specifying a desired outcome, and then making it happen."

The effectiveness of a change agent depends on his or her ability to influence others, to discover and mobilize human energy (both in him/herself and in other employees), to maintain a sense of humor and perspective and to have self-confidence and interpersonal skills (Burke, 1992). Although most of these skills can be learned, individuals who during a change process make the transition from manager to change agent often encounter major difficulties, since they are not prepared for the complexity, ambiguity and uncertainty specific to this project. To make the transition from manager to change agent, a prospective manager must possess the following skills:[7]

- Understand and apply the objectives of the change process
- Adopt a change agent's roles and responsibilities
- Design and develop the change activities
- Demonstrate competencies and skills specific to a change agent
- Implement and evaluate change initiatives

An efficient change agent must possess all the necessary abilities and capabilities to initiate and successfully manage an organizational change process. The change agent should have enough knowledge in managing change along with social psychology and display communication skills,

---

[7] Gilley J. W. (2001), *The Manager as Change Agent: A Practical Guide to Developing High Performance, People and Organizations,* Basic Books, pp. 5-6.

creativity and last, but not least, credibility.[8] Gaining employees' trust is not an easy task which is why the change agent must communicate with them constantly or as much as possible, trying to convince them of the necessity of the new changes, as well as presenting the potential benefits of the change.

The change agent who attempts to implement a new change can come either from within or outside the organization. Both possibilities have their advantages and disadvantages. In case of small scale changes, management usually employs someone who is a manager from within the organization and who has earned the respect and trust of others. However, when a major change is implemented, it is advised to form mixed teams of specialists with managers from within the organization and also external consultants. Thus, the experience and objectivity of external change agents is combined with the confidence and knowledge held by the internal change agents. The external consultants are more objective about the organization's situation, while the insiders have the employees' trust, being permanently in contact with them. A successful collaboration, however, is guaranteed only when the two teams get along well. And so, the change agent(s) can be either a manager or group of managers from within the organization, specialists from outside the organization, or a joint team of experts with specialists from inside and outside the company.

Following the definition of the term change agent, it is important to introduce another force that could potentially generate resistance to change—the change agent him/herself. I am referring especially to the person who is given the position of change agent when he or she identifies with a manager or group of managers from a medium or higher level of the organizational pyramid. Since usually a middle or top manager is deemed a change agent, depending of course on the magnitude of the change, I will emphasize why it is better that the chosen change agent be a person from a higher level in the organizational hierarchy.

---

[8] Predișcan Mariana (2004), *Organizational Change: What, When and How to Change,* West University Publisher, Timișoara, pp. 230-232.

I highlighted these two levels because when a new change is proposed, the organization's management usually selects a person from these categories. The course of selection differs, depending on the type and stretch of the change. The bigger the stretch of change, the better it is to choose a person, in this case a manager, from a higher level of management. Why? People usually have greater confidence in top managers, especially in those who have seniority, trusting them more even in turbulent times.

Studies have shown that middle managers can be both change agents, leading the change effort (Luscher and Lewis, 2008; Wooldridge et al., 2008), as well as change beneficiaries, resisting change initiatives (Feldman, 2004; Thomas and Linstead, 2002).

As Smith (1982) and Spreitzer and Quinn (1996) announce, executive managers and all those who have some power in the organization usually are reluctant to new changes, representing an important factor that impedes change. They prefer maintaining the current status quo to the detriment of more radical changes. "Those who usually want new changes are middle and bottom managers, while executive ones usually oppose."[9] In such cases, we can no longer discuss a planned change, initiated by top management, but by their subordinates. As resistance can manifest at all levels, we consider that it would be a mistake to focus only on the resistance manifested in top to bottom changes. Since not all changes that are proposed to be implemented are beneficial, resistance from the part of middle managers and some top managers appears as a natural reaction.

Indeed, executive managers will never oppose their own ideas but the situation is different when these ideas come from shareholders or their subordinates. First, when the change decision comes from shareholders, executive managers either obey or they leave the organization. Usually when a middle or an executive manager is chosen to be a change agent, he or she is expected to perform well in all duties. Despite that, there are cases when a change agent adopts an inappropriate management

---

[9] Predican Mariana, Braduțanu Daniela (2012), *Change Agent – A Force Generating Resistance To Change Within An Organization?*, ACTA UNIVERSITATIS DANUBIUS, Vol. 8, No. 6, pp. 8.

style, making obvious mistakes during the change process. They may not perceive employees' resistance, do not understand the reasons why employees oppose new changes, or do not know and apply efficiently the reducing resistance to change methods. "Change agents contribute to the occurrence of what they call 'resistant behaviors and communications' through their own actions and inactions, owing to their own ignorance, incompetence, or mismanagement (Ford et al., 2008: 362)." The possible actions of the change agent are communicating inadequate and inaccurate information along with misleading and betraying the employees' trust. As Cobb et al. (1995) state, change agents contribute to the increase of the resistance to change phenomenon from the part of the affected members "by breaking agreements both before and during change and by failing to restore the subsequent loss of trust." Secondly, considering that they know better what to do and to not jeopardize their authority, often change agents ignore the ideas and proposals of the affected members which leads to a further increase of resistance from the employee.

If change agents expect the resistance to change phenomenon to be manifested, then they most likely will encounter it (Kanter et al., 1992). Starting from the preconception that employees will manifest resistance, change agents will look for signs to confirm their initial assumptions. Since each change agent perceives resistance to change in his/her own way, in order to confirm his hypothesis, the change agent can classify as resistant those actions and nonactions that in reality are just normal behaviors. It is normal when a change initiative is announced for people to be curious and ask questions. They want to know more about the change process and it would be a mistake to consider such type of behavior as resistant. Change agents should try to answer all the questions and involve the employees as much as possible in the process in order to gain their support.

Sometimes, in the case of an unexpected problem, the change agent may attribute the negative effects of the change process to the resistance to change phenomenon but always, when a change will be successfully implemented, the success will belong to his or her efforts. From this point of view, resistance to change is often presented as being the source of all problems encountered in an organizational change process. In this way, change agents can transfer their own failures, as a result of some inappropriate decisions, onto the employees who manifest contention, blaming them for the failure of the change process.

Further to these considerations, I will present two ways through which the change agent can encourage resistance to change (Ford et al., 2008: 366).

> **Inappropriate communication of the need for change**

The change agent can represent a force that contributes to the increase of the resistance to change phenomenon when the need for change is communicated inappropriately. The actions through which the change agent can increase employees' resistance are through failing to justify the need for change, misrepresenting the change outcomes or by the inability to engage in the process all of the affected members of the organization.

Before getting involved in a change process, the affected members need to understand the need for change. The role of the change agent is to communicate clearly the need for change and in order to gain their support, to properly motivate the employees. It is essential for the change agent to gain employees' trust. Of course, some will ask questions. The change agent has to be prepared to answer all the questions and in those cases when he does not know the exact answers, to write down the questions, assuring employees that at the next meeting the answers will be provided. If at the next meeting the answers are not presented, the change agent's credibility might be undermined. Since the change agent does not have all the necessary information about the process, some employees might consider him unable to implement the new change, loosing their trust. The inoculation theory suggests that change agents who will not be able to generate convincing arguments to support their point of view, will end up increasing employees' immunity to change.

Another mistake often made by the change agents is noted by Larson and Tompkins (2005), the authors arguing that change agents can be ambivalent. In an attempt to present the new change, they use the plans and techniques from previous processes. Instead of focusing on the new change, they highlight the effects of the previous ones. In this way, employees are misled.

> **Misrepresentation**

Sometimes, to convince employees to participate in a change process or simply to "look good", the change agent can intentionally distort the information. The change agent typically uses this technique when he or she expects employees to react negatively to a change decision.

A more favorable presentation of a change proposal, however, is not always made intentionally. According to Lovallo and Kahneman (2003), "since decision makers have a bias toward optimism" they have a tendency to see things in a positive way. As a result, they will emphasize the positive aspects and minimize or totally ignore the negative ones. During the process and especially at the end, comparing the final results with the expected ones, some employees may have the feeling that they have been manipulated and even lied to. Their resistance will increase, and employees lose their trust and become more cautious regarding future changes.

To gain the employees' confidence, change agents must provide accurate and realistic information. The presentation of both positive and negative aspects can reduce employees' uncertainty regarding the success of the new change process and increase their confidence in the change agent.

Research shows that change agents who are honest, admit their mistakes, and those that try to restore the relations with the members involved in the process from the beginning and during the change process, will encounter a much lower resistance to change compared to those who will not do so (Cobb et al., 1995, Folger and Skarlicki, 1999).

II. Organizational environment

Organizations are usually more effective when undertaking routine activities and less effective when performing an activity for the first time and this can create a powerful defense system towards change. The second category of the forces that generate resistance to change within an organization is outlined below, each force being described separately.

Organizational Culture

The culture of any organization is unique and is shaped by the values, beliefs and assumptions of the members forming the organization. It ensures the maintenance of a certain continuity and stability for the organization's members. Therefore, any change that may cause discontinuity and instability will be met with resistance.

It is well known that companies with a strong organizational culture use human resources more efficiently. One of the strongest motivators of a person is the desire to identify with the organization and to be part of its team. According to Maslow's pyramid, once a person's needs are met from the lower levels, higher level needs of achieving a certain status, obtaining a colleague's appreciation and other matters related to intrinsic motivation are sought after. Although employees attach more importance to extrinsic motivation, after they gain more experience, its importance decreases and employees then focus more on intrinsic motivation.[10] Depending on the promoted culture, organizations will have either supportive change employees or change opponents.

The organizational culture determines a predictable behavior. As all members of an organization share the same values, it is expected that when a new change is implemented that does not correspond with their values all of the members will oppose it. In some cases, the organizational culture can represent the cause of the resistance to change phenomenon. It makes sense that any change that is contrary to the generally accepted norms and practices of the organization is met with resistance. Thus,

---

[10] Braduțanu Daniela (2011), *Identifying Motivational Factors within a Multinational Company,* ACTA UNIVERSITATIS DANUBIUS Vol. 7, No. 4, pp. 230.

thanks to a rigid culture, the organization itself can generate resistance to change.

Although organizational culture is an external factor in relation to the persons involved in an organizational change process, it influences significantly their attitudes towards change. The organizational culture is the invisible force of each company that provides coherence for the daily activities and explains why relatively similar enterprises in terms of size, market share or field obtain different results in the same market conditions.[11] Depending on the values and practices that an organizational culture is centered around, the company will either succeed or fail with an effective change implementation. Similar companies obtain different results due to the culture they practice. Thus, companies that possess an organizational culture focused on innovation and performance achievement will have employees with a positive change attitude. Resistance in such organizations will be reduced or even nonexistent. In contrast, however, are the organizations with a "conservative" culture for which the concept of innovation is unknown. Employees are accustomed to execute their tasks according to the daily routine and any change attempt is met with a lack of enthusiasm.

We can conclude that an organization's culture plays a vital role in reducing reluctance to change. In order to understand the behavior of people willing to participate or oppose a change process, the change agent must first analyze their values and beliefs. Most of the time people do not act according to reality, but rather according to their own perceptions and those employees who hold values oriented towards personal growth and creativity will be more open to change.[12] As a result, the management that promotes and emphasizes employees' personal development and performance achievement will most often enjoy a higher support from their side.

Also, in order to have supportive change employees, the organization's management must create a climate of trust within the

---

[11] Cercel M. (2012), *The Organizational Culture of Performant Companies, Doctorate Thesis*, Craiova, pp. 10.

[12] Hultman K. (1998), *Making Change Irresistable: Overcoming Resistance to Change in Your Organization*, Davies – Black Publishing, Palo Alto, California, pp. 36.

company. Once trust is part of the organization's culture, the manifestation of the resistance to change phenomenon will be reduced. The existence of a high level of trust both among members of a team or department, and between the change agent and the other members involved in the change process, is essential if a successful implementation is desired. To contribute to the success of the organization, employees must have self-confidence, trust the other team members they interact with, feel they are part of the team, and know that their skills are recognized. The existence of a high degree of trust in the organization will foster the availability for change, while distrust will foster resistance to change (Hultman, 1998: 156).

Organizational Structure

At the organization level, the structural variables can cause the appearance of the resistance to change phenomenon. Depending on the organizational structure that is used, the phenomenon's manifestation may be more or less intense. The organization must be seen as a system composed of subsystems that meet the organization's functions, act in correlation with each other and not least, respond to a decision-making hierarchy. The activity of designing or redesigning an organizational structure is complex, involving changes in the distribution of the decisional factors for which a detailed examination of the entire organization is required.

In some cases, thanks to the adoption of a rigid organizational structure, the organization itself may generate unfavorable elements towards change. In order to function effectively, the organization needs stability and continuity, but the use of a rigid structure and establishments of authority hierarchies may require that employees use only certain communication channels. The more the organization is rigid and has several levels, the greater the distance the information has to travel. And of course, there is a higher probability that this structure will reject any idea of change.

An organizational structure regulates the business activities and establishes the hierarchy in which employees of a company should operate. According to Burns and Stalker (1961), there are two ideal types of organizational structure: mechanistic structure and organic structure.

In a turbulent environment, the organizations that adopt an organic structure are more effective and responsive to change. In terms of the present business environment, characterized by a high uncertainty, the organic organizations are more compatible with the economic realities. Knowledge and task control are located anywhere in the organization, and although it is considered that the organization of an organic type is more difficult to manage, its control range is much wider with the information flowing easier.

In contrast with the organic organizations are the mechanistic ones, characteristic of a stable environment. By design, these structures are more resistant to change and have difficulties in adjusting to everything new. Employees who carry out their activities in such a structure do not have the freedom to undertake a change, must act only in a certain manner and exhibit the inability to adapt or change leading to inertia.

In conclusion organizations with a mechanistic structure will generate a greater opposition towards change than those with an organic structure. Also, depending on the economic situation, some organizations can make the transition from mechanistic structures to organic ones and conversely, the determinant being the business environment. In order to improve communication at the organizational level and to increase employees' responsibilities, the organic structure is welcome. Managers who adopt it often resort to delegation, giving more autonomy to their subordinates. Thus, employees "feel" that they are part of the process and as a result, show less resistance to change.

Management Style

The management style that a manager adopts represents the way in which he or she will further influence subordinates. As a result, employees' resistance will be greatly influenced by the embraced management style.

The best-known classification of management styles is: authoritarian, democratic, and permissive (laissez-faire). The authoritarian style, which is result-oriented, and the participatory style, which is geared towards human relations, are the two styles most often encountered in practice.

Before proceeding further, I consider it necessary to define and present some defining characteristics of the two styles.

The authoritarian management style represents the classic approach where the manager is the one who has both the power and authority to make the needed decisions. Once the decision has been made, it is communicated to the lower level employees, without the opportunity for them to express their views. An important feature of this style is that both employee motivation and influence is achieved either through a reward or a punishment. As a result of extensive research it was found that organizations that have many authoritarian managers record both a very high turnover, as well as a high degree of absenteeism from their employees (Ispas, 2012).

Authors like Muczyk and Reimann (1987), Yukl (1989) and Bass (1981), state that this management style is task-oriented, having a persuasive and manipulative character (in Clark et al., 2009: 212). Depending on the employees' attitudes and mindsets, the adoption of this style can be beneficial or detrimental. It is not recommended to embrace the authoritarian style if employees feel stressed, have a high reliance on a manager and are not able to generate creative ideas, as well as in those situations where they want to be actively involved in the organizational change processes taking place within the organization. On the other hand, adopting this style can be beneficial in situations where new staff is hired and the employees are not familiar with the procedures or if they lack sufficient knowledge to execute their tasks. Furthermore, it is best employed when the time to make a change decision is limited, an imposed or urgent change is required to be implemented, or when employees do not have sufficient experience to make decisions (Zlate, 2004: 101-137).

The participatory management style, which is also called democratic, is characterized by employee involvement in the decision-making process, whereby the employees are encouraged to express their opinions and to make contributions that could benefit, in this case, the change process. The authors Clark et al. (2009: 213) state that employees who are working with a manager who adopts a participatory style tend to be more involved, committed and loyal than those working alongside an authoritarian manager.

Delegation and staff support are basic characteristics of this management style, an emphasis being placed on teamwork and employee's freedom to make decisions. There are cases, however, where the adoption of this style is not recommended, particularily when the organization's management does not have enough time to learn the views of all employees, when the manager feels threatened by the employee's involvement and/or when no mistakes or delays are admitted in the process (Zlate, 2004: 101-137).

In comparing the two management styles we can conclude that reluctance to change will be much higher in those cases where the manager practices an authoritarian style, characteristic to a collectivist culture, versus the manager who adopts a participative style, specific to an individualistic culture.

Researching the literature, I found that in order to successfully implement an organizational change process it is not recommended to use only a certain management style, but a combination of the above-mentioned approaches. Of course, each manager will choose the style that characterizes him or her better and which is considered appropriate for each specific situation. As Robert Tannenbaum and Warren Schmidt enunciated in the article "How to Choose a Leadership Pattern", published by Harvard Business Review in 1957, "the leadership style is the manager's *option.*"

An effective manager must be able to adapt a management style according to each situation. In chapter V, I will present that the position of the reducing resistance to change stage differs depending on the type of organizational change that follows the implementation. As a result, the management style that will be embraced will also be different depending on the type of change.

In case of a planned or incremental change, the participatory management style is recommended. Resistance to change must be reduced before the actual implementation of the change which is why managers need to constantly communicate with employees and involve them as much as possible in the process, thus earning their trust and commitment. Năstase (2006: 29) states that managers who will encourage a participatory environment in their organization will enjoy a much higher level of involvement from their employees. They will become more responsible and the degree of attachment towards their superiors and the organization will amplify considerably.

In case of urgent or imposed changes, when the change decision needs to be taken quickly and the manager or the change agent does not have enough time to prepare employees, it is advisable to adopt an authoritarian management style. The decision made by organization's management is imposed on all employees and in this case it is recommended that both during implementation and at the end, managers try to explain the reasons for this immediate decision and to involve the employees step by step in the process.

From a personal point of view, I believe that an effective manager should not use only one management style, but a combination of the above-outlined styles with a greater propensity towards the participatory one. The more employees feel that they are part of the change process and their ideas matter, resistance to change will be very low or even nonexistent because people rarely oppose their own ideas and contributions. A rapid transition from the authoritarian style to a participatory one is difficult, especially if there are conservative managers who are "afraid" to delegate tasks and worry about losing the power and authority they have. This often leads to an increased resistance to change and, in many cases, the failure of the attempted change. At the same time, I believe that a certain degree of authority must exist, since the organization's top management has much more knowledge and information about the future trajectory of the organization and what improvements are beneficial and necessary. Most times, when deciding a change, employees focus only on their personal interests, while executive managers have a global vision, placing the company's interests first.

Personnel Policy

Another force generating resistance to change is represented by the organization's personnel policy. This policy refers to the rules pertaining to recruiting, hiring, training, remunerating and promoting employees. Depending on the existing personnel policy within an organization, resistance to change from the employees will be either reduced or increased.

The policy is developed by the organization's management and addresses all hierarchical levels. Depending on the established policy and the compliance with its components, companies will have competent and proficient employees who will contribute to the achievement of organizational goals.

The components of the personnel policy are:

- Selection and recruitment
- Motivation and reward
- Training
- Promotion
- Assessment

Since human potential is one of the most precious values an organization has, the success of the latter highly depends on the degree of the staff's involvement in achieving organizational goals. Nowadays it is almost impossible for a company to enjoy an upward trend in business if it does not have a highly qualified personnel oriented towards change and innovation. According to the promoted personnel policy, organizations will have employees who support change or employees who are against change.

The first component of the personnel policy is *employee selection and recruitment.* The most important selection criteria include individuals who possess leadership skills and a great capacity to adapt to new working conditions which includes risk-taking and a high tolerance of ambiguity, as well as those with skills and competences to work effectively in a team. When recruiting new employees, the human resource manager should analyze the employees' technical knowledge and skills and the compatiblity of their values and attitudes with the organizational culture.

The ability to change the existing personnel of an organization is limited, since employees will resist all processes considered damaging. Therefore, hiring new employees is welcome. Employing new staff with positive attitudes towards change and those who are eager to develop their professional skills will represent a positive aspect for innovative organizations, as the resistance to change phenomenon will be almost absent. On the other hand, when these types of companies recruit employees accustomed to executing a routine work or which have a negative attitude towards change, resistance to change will be very high. As a result, depending on the organization's type, the selection and recruitment policy must be adjusted with the organization's culture.

The motivation and reward policy refers to the opportunity of influencing employees to behave in a certain way, usually to maintain or improve productivity and then rewarding employees for their efforts. In an unstable environment, the resistance to change phenomenon is manifested more assertively and so managers must identify effective ways to motivate and reward their staff. Although for a long time the focus was just on financial grounds, at present, in particular due to the limited financial resources, the nonfinancial motivation receives increased attention. The nonfinancial motivation does not exclude the financial one, but requires employees' involvement in the organization's projects, thereby attempting to obtain a commitment, namely, employee loyalty and trust. In order to have pro change employees, managers need to adjust the motivation and reward policy based on the business environment and their employees' aspirations.

Training is another element of the personnel policy, which in the new business environment "should become permanent" (Sărătean, 2003). To cope with ongoing changes, employees should always be informed of any new changes taking place in their field and to possess the required knowledge to be able to operate under new procedures. An organizational change is implemented with much less effort when employees know what is going to occur and they are ready and able to generate creative ideas. The more the organization provides training sessions for their employees, the more these employees will be prepared to face the new processes and to be more confident in their own skills, thus showing less resistance.

Another important aspect to be considered is *employee promotion*. Typically, a higher position represents a positive move with favorable effects on employees. But seen from another perspective, for the employee who is used to executing his routine tasks and who does not like to assume any responsibilities, a new job represents the unknown, which might encourage him to oppose the promotion. Depending on personal characteristics, some people like challenges and gladly assume new risks and responsibilities, while others are more reticent, opting for a more stable environment.

Employee assessment policy is also an important component that needs to be paid attention to because it must respond to the organization's needs, without overlooking employees' expectations. Reconsideration of the evaluation system may have a strong influence on employee behavior (Clarke : 2002). It is well known that an organization establishes its reward policy based on the correlation between employee competence, behavior and achieved performance. As a result only those behaviors perceived to be favorable to the organization will be rewarded. From this perspective, it is very important to set precise employee assessment criteria and communicate this to everyone being evaluated. This includes providing the roles expected of each employee, as well as the types of behavior considered favorable for achieving the desired performance level.

Working in an increasingly turbulent and complex business environment, organizations need to take the necessary measures in order to survive. Of course, increasing organizational flexibility, decentralization and teamwork have become indispensable. In this context, in order to reduce employees' resistance to change and gain their support, the assessment system needs to be amended. Along with top-down assessment, the introduction of new criteria is required: self-evaluation, peer evaluation and bottom-up evaluation. The introduction of new criteria in the evaluation system shows the importance the organization attaches to innovation, adaptation to new changes, teamwork and the correlation of the appraisal system with the reward policy, training and rewarding staff. After all, it is essential if a successful change implementation is desired to recognize those with a favorable attitude towards change.

In the situation where a company's personnel policy does not contain all the necessary elements or some of them are not complied with by management, it may represent an important force generating resistance. It is recommended that when the human resource manager elaborates the organization's personnel policy, to consider the aspects related to the industry and environment in which it operates. In order to have pro change employees and be able to operate in uncertain and turbulent environments, the formulated personnel policy must include the above-listed elements, focusing in particular on training, motivation and an appropriate reward. Also, to benefit from less resistance, everyone in the company who holds decision power positions should ensure that their subordinates are taken care of.

In conclusion, an effective change implementation is not possible without an appropriate adjustment of the organization's personnel policy. Since the success of a new change depends on how employees react, management should pay more attention when formulating the personnel policy. Otherwise, if it is not elaborated effectively, it can recruit employees whose attitudes and values do not match those of the organization and, as a result, they will oppose any change decision. Of course, the more that employees will be trained and be "compatible" with the organization's requirements, the less resistance there will be.

Information System

The information system is a key aspect of the management function. Without a well-defined information system, managers cannot influence their subordinates to act in order to achieve the desired performance and they cannot properly inform them about what is taking place or will take place in the organization.

The quality and quantity of information that members of an organization receive from change agents will decisively influence their degree of resistance. Employees involved in an organizational change process will oppose a higher resistance when the organization's information system will not allow an efficient movement of information from the executive management towards themselves.

To reduce this reluctance to change and to obtain employees' support, an open and honest communication from the change agent is required. The agent must communicate clearly and by all available means of communication what will take place and what effects the new change will generate. Of course, the more rigid and multi-leveled the organization, the longer will be the road the information has to travel. Thus, there is a high probability that the information that will reach the recipients will be modified, as it depends on the transmitter's subjectivity. In such cases, it is recommended to have a feedback system showing how the information travels properly through the route transmitter - receiver. Also, the manager or the change agent who understands and uses the communication channels appropriately, both formal and informal, is more able to identify the potential barriers existing in the information system and to take the necessary steps to overcome and improve them.

If in the past, this reluctance to change could arise from technical communication difficulties (a total or partial absence of efficient telecommunication systems or their low reliability), at present, this impediment is significantly diminished due to multiple communication technologies (email, fax, and mobile) and their increased reliability and efficiency. Thus, it becomes evident that today resistance to change is more often generated by the lack of communication and not by the communication channels.

However, there are exceptions. If managers today have a wide range of means of information production, there were enough situations where managers indicated clashes with their delay, loss or distortion. Focusing more and more on the introduction of new technologies in order to improve organizational performance, some managers have neglected their effectiveness.

Over-industrialization and an increasing reliance on modern telecommunication systems could cause massive financial losses. One example is the computerized information system of stock exchanges. Due to the computer system failure that showed the price of the stocks in real time, on April 5, 2000, the opening of the London Stock Exchange was delayed by aproximately eight hours. In June 2005, in New Zealand, a similar event took place, when two telecommunication cables simultaneously failed, causing the stock market to stop its activity for five hours. Also, in June 2008, due to some problems with the trading system, the Oslo Stock Exchange opened with a delay of five and a half hours. These events have caused rapid responses from many banks and brokers around the globe, with adverse effects on stock prices.

Although the above examples relate primarily to significant financial losses due to temporary interruptions of telecommunication systems, we can understand how resistance to change can occur due to the technical failure of telecommunication systems that do not allow (temporarily) the communication of this important information.

III. Economic environment

The economic environment is another force generating reluctance to change that through its evolution influences the behavior of the organization and its employees. Depending on the state of the economic environment, employees will exhibit a lower or higher degree of reluctance.

Most organizations adapt their activities according to the economic environment. If the economy is growing, organizations can expand their activities as there are more jobs available, with more opportunities for employees. As a result, opposition to change will be much higher as employees will have more employment options. A fast growing economy, a low unemployment and inflation rate, a reduced share of bad loans in total loans, as well as a high purchasing power of the population, are indicators that will determine a higher degree of resistance to change. On the contrary are the situations when the economy is in recession and registering negative values. In such cases, employees' opposition to change will be much reduced or even absent, as they will try to keep their jobs by any means and show support towards the management's decisions. Thus, employees' resistance to change will be much lower when the unemployment rate is high and the pace of economic development is low and recording even negative values. This will also be the case when the economy is in recession, the number of available jobs is very low, the inflation rate is high and recording a rising trend, the share of bad loans is high and has a tendency to increase in total loans, and the purchasing power of the population is increasingly reduced.[13]

In conclusion, employees will show a greater resistance to change during a favorable economic environment and with an upward trend, than in situations of unstable economy or recession.

---

[13] Predişcan Mariana, Braduțanu Daniela, Roiban Roxana Nadina (2013), *Forces that Enhance or Reduce Employee Resistance to Change*, 9th edition of the International Conference "European Integration – New Challenges", 24-25 May, University of Oradea.

Reducing Resistance to Change Methods

In this chapter I will present and detail some of the most representative methods to reduce resistance to change. Analyzing the literature, I have decided to describe nine methods that I consider will efficiently reduce the resistance to change phenomenon if they are applied properly.

The proposed methods are continuous communication, involvement, traning, delegation, positive motivation, counseling and support, negotiation, hidden persuasion, and explicit and implicit coercion.

Continuous Communication

Communication is one of the most effective ways to reduce reluctance to change because when employees know what occurs in the organization, they are more willing to express their support and join the process. Many times, the determinant for resistance to change for individuals and groups is the inadequate information or lack of it.

Lacking knowledge regarding what is happening or is about to happen in the organization, employees cannot decide on which side of the fence they are standing. Since most often a new implemention brings new modifications, interrupting the staff's daily routine, employees are more likely to manifest opposition.

In times of change, members of the organization are less confident, especially those who in the past have had negative experiences. In order to gain their commitment to change, managers must provide sufficient information to employees so they feel "in charge" of the situation.

Constant communication helps people understand the need for change, how it will occur and what will be the probable consequences. In any organizational change process there are two statements that are often heard. First, the staff affected by the change will declare that "they did not receive sufficient information and the management did not communicate what occurs in the organization" and secondly, the change agent, namely the one dealing with implementing a change, will state that "he has consistently spread the held information", with the explanation that "he has only communicated the information that could be disclosed at the time."

I believe that continuous communication is an effective way of reducing resistance to change for the affected members, so that the change agents can present their information and the members have the opportunity to express their views. An important reason why employees resist a new change is concern about their own interests. Because of this, people often will ask questions, but I want to emphasize that not always those who ask the most questions are the most resistant. In their own way, people are curious about things that are new. They want details on what will happen next, how the new change will affect them and what the potential benefits are. Managers must be able to provide accurate information regarding the starting date of the change process, as well as how it will unfold. By communicating accurate and appropriate data, including the potential losses and benefits, the change agent has a good chance of winning employees' trust.

Research shows that as a result of a broken trust or betrayal, "people will lower their productivity, reduce their work quality, become uncooperative, or, in extreme cases, seek revenge or retaliation through sabotage, theft."[14] Having lost faith in the change leaders, employees

---

[14] Ford J. D., Ford Laurie W. (2010), *Stop Blaming Resistance to Change and Start Using It*, Organizational Dynamics, Vol. 39, No. 1, pp. 33.

will need a sincere apology and facts that prove that the leaders are willing to correct their mistakes. According to some studies, when managers express their mistakes publicly and apologize, employees are more likely to show their empathy and respect (Ford and Ford, 2010; Cobb et al., 1995; Folger and Skarlicki, 1999). A manager's credibility increases as employees understand that nobody is perfect and to err is human.

Today, many contemporary organizations have learned that in order to survive in the marketplace and to be efficient, they must constantly communicate with and involve their members in the processes that are taking place. The obsessive secrecy of the large companies in terms of strategy and competition can generate more internal costs than external benefits. It is essential that managers from all organizational levels, particularly those from the lower levels know and understand the need, the logic, and the effects of new change processes. I stressed the importance of the role of the lower levels managers because they are the ones who interact with employees from the bottom levels of the organizational pyramid and they are more influential in how pronounced the employees' resistance will be.

The major problem faced by many organizations in the current period is not whether or not managers engage in a communication process, but how information is communicated either satisfactorily or unsatisfactorily to the other members. So that the affected members better understand the views of those who initiate a change, it is recommended that the relations between the two sides be an open, two-way communication.

In an organization, communication among different departments and between employees is done through written and oral communication tools. The means of written communication most often used are e-mail, fax, and mail. These methods of communication involve the mastery of specific skills held by employees, that they are capable of writing clear and concise messages, well-structured and without grammatical errors. Following some studies done by US companies, it was found that the largest problem related to employees' skills was written communication.

Unlike written communication, verbal communication is less formal, involving an interactive relationship between two or more people. As an advantage, verbal communication is much faster, employee's feedback can be obtained instantly, but as a disadvantage, the verbal transmission of a message from one person to another can be misinterpreted, leading to distortion of its content and meaning. Verbal communication is not always the most effective way of communication since it is influenced by factors related to paraverbal language (tone, volume, rate of speech) and body language (facial expression, body position and movement). In order to ensure an effective communication between the change initiators and the affected members, and to reduce possible misunderstandings, I recommend combining the two types of communication.

Involvement

In order to reduce reluctance to change, employees need to be both involved in the change process and supported by the organization's leadership throughout it. Involving employees in the process helps reduce their reluctance by reducing anxiety, creating a strong sense of ownership about change and allowing individuals to actively contribute to shaping the change (Peccei et al., 2011: 190).

When employees are involved in decision making, they not only have an important contribution to make, but they also better understand the rationale of the new changes for themselves. This leads to greater motivation and putting forth additional effort from their side, which results in accepting better decisions at the organizational level (Brown and Cregan, 2008: 672). Involving the affected personnel in the change process from the start contributes to the creation of synergy and commitment at all organizational levels. Every organization should have an employee involvement program integrated into its culture, representing a self-driven process, whose purpose would be making the employees accountable.[15]

---

[15] Kauffman C. (2010), *Employee Involvement: A New Blueprint for Success*, Journal of Accountancy, May, pp. 49.

If change agents desire to obtain the employees' commitment, they should involve them in the process starting with the planning stage. In order to grant full support, employees must "feel" that they are part of the process, contributing with ideas that are taken into consideration by their superiors. It is recommended that employees be involved in all stages of an organizational change process, starting with the change's planning or design, continuing with its implementation and ending with evaluating its effectiveness.

People naturally will oppose changes they do not understand or do not consider important. Since this reluctance is usually related to the values, beliefs and change responses from the individual's side, it follows that the phenomenon is actually an inevitable and integral part of any organizational change process (Hynds, 2010: 378). In order to give their support, employees must understand the need for change, be confident that they can cope with it and trust the change agent.

Middle and lower level managers are the closest to employees, playing a key role in implementing a new change. According to Prosci (2012), middle level management was identified in some studies as the most resistant group but also the most important contributor when its support was obtained. It is almost impossible for a change process to be successfully implemented if middle level managers resist or do not get involved, or simply do not believe in its success. For this reason, the change agent must act very carefully, identifying middle managers position from the start.

The role of the middle managers is very important in an organizational change process, especially when the change decision is undertaken by top managers. Before starting the process, top management should ensure that the middle level managers have all the necessary information to initiate the change and are on their side. This aspect is very important, as the middle level managers will be the ones to negotiate with both sides, conveying decisions from higher levels to lower levels, respectively, and communicating suggestions and proposals for improvement from lower levels to the top. Since the middle and lower level managers will be the ones interacting directly with the employees from the bottom level of the organizational pyramid, it is recommended for them to be pro change supporters of the process otherwise, instead of creating an atmosphere of trust and commitment towards change, they will contribute to the increase of resistance.

In every department of an organization exists an informal leader whose opinions and advice are often requested by other members. In order to expedite the personnel's commitment, it is recommended that managers obtain first the support of the informal leaders. Involving informal leaders in the change process from the planning stage and asking their opinions and ideas for better implementation will surely lead to a pro change attitude from their side. This favorable attitude towards change will be observed by the other members of the organization, who having trust in their leaders, will follow them and in turn get involved in the process.

Involving the affected members in the organizational change process has many advantages by allowing them to have the opportunity to contribute with new ideas to improve the process. It is well known that normal circumstances do not necessarily bring out the best in people, while crises situations do. Only by being part of the process can employees better understand the importance of the new changes and the future benefits they will enjoy. It should not be overlooked, however, that the participation method is recommended to be practiced only if employees manifest a desire to get involved. There were multiple cases when employees did not want to get involved, but they were forced by management, which led to resentment against the supervisor (Galle and Leahy, 2009) and the employees quickly become discouraged if the group leader dominated the decision-making process (Siddique et al., 2011).

Training

Everything new is associated with some uncertainty. To cope with new situations and often new technologies, employees require appropriate training. It is critical that the organization's management ensure its staff proper preparation, so that they have specific tools and knowledge to cope with the new change (Kotter, 1995; Kumar et al., 2007).

In current market conditions, employee training has become a necessity. In order to develop and "survive" in a continuous changing market, companies need people who are capable, creative, efficient, and open to new challenges. For this reason, many organizations use the services of training companies whose purpose is to train employees so that they can maintain or increase productivity and/ or perform new activities.

Employees resist new change because of two important reasons: loss of control, the determinant being fear of incompetence, and the effect of surprise. In order to gain employees' confidence and diminish their fears, I recommend sending them to training courses immediately after the change process is initiated and not waiting for the whole process to be completed. Employees require some time to learn how to use the new technologies and programs, as well as to adjust to the new procedures. Also, the training courses represent an effective way of training and improving the staff's knowledge, providing both theoretical and practical courses, the latter being more interactive.

Another important aspect to be considered is the type and size of the change that is intended to be implemented and the current degree of preparedness of those affected. Depending on the type and size of the change, the duration of the training process will vary. In the case of a large scale change, whether planned or incremental, the required training period is longer because personnel needs more time to adapt to the new changes. On the contrary are the situations when the change is on a small scale, unplanned or imposed. Employees have very little time to adjust to the new changes so the training sessions are limited.

Although often it is stated that depending on the readiness of those affected, the duration of the training process will vary, in practice, these claims are not valid. In correlation with the change magnitude, the duration of the training courses will be decided. There are multiple situations when the training costs of an existing employee with a low level of preparation are much higher compared to the use of hiring a new employee. Since maintaining or reducing costs is a vital criterion for any organization, top management may resort to the tactic of bringing a well-trained employee from outside, instead of advancing an insider.

Delegation

The delegation method used more and more often by managers plays an important role in reducing opposition to change. A strong reason for its use is that through it the mutual trust between the change agents and those affected by the change is reinforced, thus creating the prerequisites for a better collaboration. The active involvement of both parties in the process contributes to better communication and information sharing, with positive effects regarding the change.

Delegation represents the transfer of the decision-making power from one person of a higher hierarchical level to another of a lower hierarchical level for a limited period, the latter following to assume responsibility for the decisions that are made. An empowered employee is the one who feels an affiliation towards his/her workplace, this affiliation resulting from the ability to assume responsibility for the decisions and related consequences (Al-Ma'ani and Isma'il, 2008).

Delegation is based on the assumption that decisions do not always have to be taken by people from the top of the organizational pyramid (Galbraith, 1973; Von Simson, 1990). According to Hennestad (2002), authority should be delegated to those managers or employees who know the problem and have enough information and kept away from those who are more isolated. Indeed, employees who understand the need for change will get involved more actively in the process when they have the necessary authority to help make decisions than those who do not have sufficient information.

Companies that have delegation as an integral part of their organizational culture are characterized by more efficient communication between upper and lower levels managers, and an increased ability to respond to the environment (Abu-Jarad et al., 2010; Hennestad, 2002). Of course, the degree of delegation can vary depending on the superior's level of confidence in his/her subordinates and the organization's needs at a time. When an urgent change is required, the top management might not have enough time to delegate certain tasks, resorting to the involvement of middle and lower level managers during the implementation stage or immediately after it. Management will delegate sufficient authority to a few targeted managers whose support is essential for the success of the process and as stated by J. Forbes Farmer (2011: 22), "the authority will be delegated to a team rather than an individual." Typically, informal leaders will be given a certain degree of authority for a limited period because it is believed that if they are convinced of the need for change, they will influence the other members of the group, thus significantly reducing the group's opposition.

Delegation has multiple positive effects on the organizational level. Research shows that practicing delegation led to an increased mutual trust between managers and employees (Akbar et al., 2011; Arnetz and Blomkvist, 2007); it increased employee engagement and morale (Vasugi and Manicka, 2011), thus contributing to a reduced level of reluctance to change. Also, there is a positive correlation between delegation and involvement (Sarwar and Khalid, 2011: 666). In some studies it was found that the more employees are given decision power, the more they will get involved in the new processes, manifesting support.

However, "staff empowerment is by no means a panacea for all management problems (Forbes Farmer, 2011: 22)." A recent study shows that a large number of employees from small organizations, which have been offered the opportunity to participate in the decision-making process have not shown enough initiative and experience to take the necessary decisions, and when the manager intervened, staff's morale had declined dramatically (Yao and Cui, 2010).

In conclusion, through delegation, a large percentage of employees become involved in the change initiatives, contributing directly or indirectly to its implementation. The success of an organizational change process depends largely on employees' degree of responsibility, because if they will feel a part of the process and be able to contribute to decision making, they will engage more actively and become supporters of this change.

Positive Motivation

Working in a constantly changing environment, maintaining or increasing the organization's level of performance becomes harder and harder for many companies. In order to maintain its performance, the organization's management first must be able to keep the most valuable employees, which can mainly be achieved through proper motivation, both financial and nonfinancial. As stated by Twyla Dell (1988), the most important part of the motivation process is to give people exactly what they want from their workplace. The more top managers are able to give employees what they want, the more they can expect positive results in terms of productivity and service quality.

After identifying the causes to the opposition, the change agent must develop a plan to reduce them, specific to each category of employees. Depending on their own fears, each employee will react differently. In order to get their commitment and support, the change agent must be able to provide the exact things they need. Of course, the offered motivation may be intrinsic, extrinsic, or a combination of the two, depending on the personnel's needs at the moment of change. According to the authors Wadell and Sohal (1998), "an optimal level of motivation" from the manager is necessary, if the goal is to increase employees' attachment to change and improve outcomes.

A positive motivation has numerous advantages. The more employees perceive benefits as a result of the change, the more they will manifest positive attitudes towards the process. An appropriate motivation and reward will also help achieve the organizational goals in a shorter period and with lower efforts. The resistance to change phenomenon will be reduced or even nonexistent, as employees will be satisfied, knowing exactly what to do.

If in the past the focus was mainly on financial motivation, salary being the determinant, currently, the popularity of the nonfinancial motivation has increased considerably. Due to scarce resources, more and more organizations turn to this method, being regarded much more accessible. The question that most organization managers ask themselves is: "How can we keep employees close to the organizational values and at peak of their efficiency when volatility is high and budgets for communications and human resources almost nonexistent?" Especially in the current conditions, when many organizations are facing financial problems, managers must find creative solutions to maintain the best employees.

The main reason why people resist is their own interest. When a loss is expected as a result of a new change implementation, an employee's natural reaction will be to oppose. For this reason, alongside effective communication and employee involvement, proper motivation is required. The motivational process should address all the affected members, because the success of an organization is not found only in its product's quality and excellent management, but especially in the employee's level of commitment.

If short term top management can retain employees only through financial motivation, in the long term they will need to make a greater effort, gaining their trust and loyalty through an adequate nonfinancial motivation.

Nonfinancial motivation does not exclude the financial one, but helps the latter. It involves gaining employees' attachment and loyalty while ensuring an upward trend in the career of the best employees. The nonfinancial motivating campaigns represent "complete business tools" undertaken to help achieve organizational objectives.

Teambuilding and *special events* are two examples of nonfinancial motivators based on interactions, these being the most popular and most often practiced by managers. Teambuilding is the favored one and also the cheapest. The emphasis is placed on teamwork and the team's success or failure is reflected on all the involved members. The purpose of these interactions is to integrate the strengths of the group members so that they can be more productive and generate creative ideas that will contribute to the achievement of the organizational goals. The success of this type of nonfinancial motivation consists in attracting employees and creating a vision and practice shared by all members. Therefore, employees will be more committed to the organization and when the decision of a new change will be announced, they will understand its need and will not show opposition.

Positive motivation is a very effective way of reducing resistance to change, especially in times of crisis. A diminished consumption impacts an organization's activities, an effect that leads to a lower production, respectively, reducing head count. Of course, companies will try to take various actions to maintain their performance and market position, the success of which will depend to a large extent on the support they'll receive from the employees' side. The fear of losing their job and monthly income will represent a strong motivator for employees not to oppose the new changes, but on the contrary, to support them. Also, if in the past people were more motivated by the financial side, currently, more and more focus is placed on the nonfinancial part, namely, a stable company in a leading market in which they will have the opportunity to be promoted and develop a successful career. Despite limited financial resources, top management must motivate and reward the most valuable employees, giving them both intrinsic and extrinsic benefits.

Counseling and Support

Under an increasingly turbulent business environment, when an employee's resistance to change reason is fear of the unknown and concern about what will follow after the change will be implemented, employee counseling has become an indispensable process. Counseling is an information and evaluation technique through which a specialist attempts to change human behavior in a positive way. It is a short process with a goal of helping people overcome the obstacles faced at the time and assisting them with adapting quicker to the changing conditions.

Employee counseling can be achieved through many forms, ranging from friendly encounters outside the workplace to personal counseling sessions and from informal meetings between management and employees to official communication sessions that meet all the members affected by the change. If the latter method will be chosen, the change agent must take into account that some employees may be more timid and not acknowledge their fears and anxieties in front of the other members and so, as a result, an allocation of separate sessions with each member is recommended.

To be on the change's side and to support all the new processes, management must ensure their employees that they are supported throughout the process and their concerns are being listened to and taken into consideration. Providing support is crucial, especially if the resistance phenomenon is based on such feelings as fear and anxiety. Some managers ignore these types of resistance, underestimating this method's effectiveness. The main disadvantage of this approach is that it requires a lot of time and therefore is expensive, and often doomed. In conclusion, if the organization lacks sufficient time, money and patience, using this method does not make sense.

Negotiation

The negotiation method can represent a very useful way of reducing reluctance to change, especially in those cases where the above-mentioned methods fail or do not produce the expected results. This technique is recommended to be used when an individual or group that has the power to block a change is likely to suffer a substantial loss as a result of the change implementation (Wagner and Hollenbeck, 2010: 291). In other words, the negotiation method is suitable to be used where it is clear that someone will suffer a loss due to the new change and therefore, can manifest a strong resistance.

Most negotiations refer to distributive negotiations when the parties are more concerned with dividing the limited resources they have. However, when a new change implementation is decided, it is recommended to apply the integrative negotiation, which implies the existence of a common decision-making process, the aim being to increase the available resources in order to make subsequent distributions. In this way the relationship is a "win-win" situation.

Reaching a joint agreement represents a relatively easy way to avoid a strong resistance although, in many cases, it can be quite costly. Once the change agent has announced the decision to negotiate and make concessions, he/she may be subject to blackmail. The application of this method is considered to be effective only if the change agent manages to reach a mutual agreement with the affected members in time otherwise, the technique is consuming both time and financial resources, creating tensions within the organization.

Also, if the duration of the change implementation is long, I recommend using several methods and techniques or combinations thereof at various stages of implementation in order to reduce more effectively any member's resistance to change. The change agent is the person who will decide what methods need to be selected to reduce the staff's resistance in a period as short as possible, because interacting with the employees, the change agent is supposed to know both the reasons that underline their resistance as well as their expectations.

Hidden Persuasion

The term hidden persuasion used by Wagner and Hollenbeck (2010: 292) assumes that members of an organization can be persuaded to join a new change if some "hidden efforts" are applied. The change agent generally uses this method when others do not prove their effectiveness or are too costly. The main forms of hidden persuasion are manipulation and co-optation.

In some cases, the managers try to hide the true intentions regarding a change process, using *manipulation*: a selective communication of information and its presentation in a specific way, favorable to the change initiator. The change agent presents the situation in a more favorable way, structuring the events so they appear more attractive in order to increase the acceptance of the new process. As a result, the real situation is distorted, the change agent resorting to misleading the affected members by false arguments, passing on messages that are not true.

The affected members can be manipulated through the following types of communication with purely pathological character: disinformation, propaganda, poisoning and imposture, as well as several types of communication that include rumors, lies, advertising, and polemics. Manipulation is often used during crisis situations when other methods aren't useful and employees need to be engaged quickly. Of course, the application of this method requires a range of knowledge and skills from the change agent, as the method is effective only when the subject does not feel involved.

On the other hand, *co-optation* assumes providing to an individual or group leader the wanted role in planning and implementing a change. This is not a form of participation, because the change agent does not seek to involve the members, only to obtain their support. In certain circumstances, co-optation is a relatively cheap and convenient way of obtaining employees' support, being cheaper than negotiation and quicker than participation, but also has some disadvantages. If people feel they are being lied to and are not treated fairly, their reaction could be extremely negative. In addition, co-optation may create more problems if the co-opted employees are using their influence in a way that does not meet the organization's interests.

It is well known that most people are likely to perceive negatively what they consider lying or an unfair treatment. Moreover, if the manager or change agent will continue to use manipulation and co-optation, he risks losing the ability to use other required approaches, such as communication, training or involvement. Despite numerous disadvantages, in critical situations, when the organization's management does not have enough time to train and involve its employees, does not have sufficient financial resources to stimulate them or when the application of the other methods do not offer the desired result, the use of hidden persuasion is the only way to convince employees that the proposed change is imperative.

Explicit and Implicit Coercion

Applying coercion can virtually overcome any type of resistance to change (Wagner and Hollenbeck, 2010: 292). By its definition, coercion is a coercive measure often used by managers to urge their subordinates to fulfill a particular obligation or impose their will and ideas, using the difference of power. Basically, the change initiators can force their staff to accept a new change by threats (loss of promotion or even job), actual layoffs or a lower salary. As stated by Năstase (2009: 82), "the change initiators must understand that there is a natural tendency for people to disregard or abandon easily certain things that they need to learn or do, as are subjected to act under coercion."

Coercion is a frecquently used method in Eastern European organizations, especially in times of crisis. Top managers holding a much stronger position compared to the middle and lower level managers can afford imposing their views. Employees either adapt to the new conditions and procedures or they are demoted or fired. This method is most often used when an urgent change is required to be implemented and there is not sufficient time to communicate with, train and involve staff, when the other methods fail, or when the change initiator's position is much stronger compared to the opposing members.

The disadvantages of the practice of this method is that it generates a general feeling of dissatisfaction in the affected employees, prompting the establishment of a tense organizational climate, with negative effects on employees' morale and performance. As stated by Hultman (1998), since employees can show their support for change only when threatened, the chances that their behavior will be maintained after the threat is gone, is reduced. The author believes that coercion is not a very effective way to change a behavior, but only to achieve results at a certain time. Like hidden persuasion, the use of coercion is a risky process because people will always resist imposed changes. However, when an immediate change implementation is required and employees oppose this, coercion may be the manager's only option.

A Reducing Resistance to Change Model

Identifying the Reducing Resistance to Change Stage

The purpose of this section is to identify the reducing resistance to change stage in an organizational change process. Further I will highlight the position of this stage depending on the type of change that is intended to be implemented.

The position of the reducing resistance to change stage in the structure of an organizational change process is not the same, depending on the type of change that is desired to be implemented. Although the purpose of any change process is the transition from a current state, considered unsatisfactory, to a next one, considered desired, the process itself varies from one change to another. Depending on the change that is intended to be implemented, the resistance to change from the organization's members will be different.

There are many types of organizational changes and in order to identify and highlight the place of the reducing resistance to change stage, I will refer to some of them.

In practice, it is well known that employees are more willing to provide support for the implementation of a new strategic change when it is planned, participative, incremental and bottom-up. Employees participate more actively in the organizational change process if they feel that they are part of it and contribute to decision making. Accordingly, employees will accept a change decision with more excitement if it was suggested by them.

For the above-mentioned types of change, the reducing resistance to change stage is recommended to be placed before the actual implementation stage. The change decision must be communicated by the executive managers in advance allowing employees to have enough time to adapt to the new conditions and acquire the necessary skills to be able to perform their activities under the new changes. This positioning of the reducing resistance to change stage in an organizational change process is recommended, as to successfully implement a new change, the support and involvement of all members of the organization is essential. They need to be informed in advance about what will take place and feel that they are part of the process from the beginning, starting with the planning stage.

Although most of the changes that are implemented within an organization are planned, there are cases when the need for change occurs suddenly. Depending on the business environment, the organization's management may decide to implement an urgent change, with its success possibly impacting the future of the organization.

The urgent changes that occur "overnight", usually are unplanned, imposed, top-down and in some cases radical. The employees' reaction to this type of change will certainly be very negative, whereby the success of the implementation is impacted by the management's capacity to communicate with and motivate employees properly. In such crisis situations, when an urgent and unplanned change is required to be implemented, the change agent has no alternative but to implement it immediately. A question arises: where is the reducing resistance to change stage located?

In such situations, Mariana Predişcan[16] proposes to follow the next three steps:

1) To identify the required change

2) To implement the change

3) To reduce resistance to change

Since the change managers do not have enough time to inform the employees and to obtain their support before the implementation phase, I recommend doing so immediately after implementing the new change. Once the implementation phase has begun, the resisting forces will make their appearance and concurrently with the advancement of the process, their manifestation will increase significantly. Clearly, most of the staff will be confused, with their morale down and even indignant, reasons for which the organization's management must act quickly. For the new change to be successfully implemented, I recommend the managers to communicate constantly with their employees and actively involve them in the process, starting with the implementation phase. The role of the change agent is very important, as he/she immediately must recourse to the introduction of the reducing resistance to change stage otherwise the success of the process that has already begun might be in danger. First, the employees must be told the reasons that prompted the immediate change implementation and secondly, they must be informed of the advantages that they will benefit from.

From the above, we can summarize that the reducing resistance to change stage can be applied both before and after the implementation phase. Depending on the organization's particularities and the type of change, the organization's management will have to decide which is the right moment for unrolling the reducing resistance to change actions.

Analyzing several organizational change models existing in the literature, I have found that the reducing resistance to change stage is present, absent, or inferred through the proposed reducing resistance to the change methods.

---

[16] Predişcan Mariana, Săcui Violeta (2011), *Opportunity to Reduce Resistance to Change in A Process of Organizational Change*, The Annals of the University of Oradea, Section Economic Sciences, Vol. II, TOM XX, pp. 697-793.

In the following table I have presented a summary of the organizational change models, the places given respectively to the reducing resistance to change stage.

Identification of the reducing resistance to change stage within an organizational change model

The reducing resistance to change stage is present	The reducing resistance to change stage is absent	The reducing resistance to change stage can be inferred
Prediṣcan's Model	Lewin's Model	Edgar Huse's Model
John Sena's Model	Moorhead – Griffin's Model	Rosabeth Moss Kanter's Model
	Beckhard and Harris's Model	John Kotter's Model
	Florescu – Popescu's Model	Tichy and Devanna's Model
		Nadler and Tushman's Model

From the above table we can easily see that only two organizational change models, Prediṣcan's Model and John Sena's Model, enjoy the explicit presence of the reducing resistance to change stage. This stage is clearly defined and in order to ensure the success of the new change, the authors located it before the implementation phase. Before making a change, employees must be informed, educated and actively involved in the process, feeling that they are contributing and are part of it. Usually, everything that is new is associated either with a potential gain or a potential loss. Therefore, a proper motivation and presentation of the advantages employees will benefit further from are elemental. The main ways of reducing resistance to change recommended by John Sena in his model are through patience, education and communication.

In Prediṣcan's Model, the second phase of the projection's stage is entitled "reducing resistance to change". The author puts great emphasis on this stage because "if people do not want to change and act accordingly to the new standards, the new change will not likely last." The main ways recommended in this model for an effective reduction of resistance to change are through employee information and motivation.

An important aspect of Predişcan's Model is that although it applies to planned strategic changes, the model can be adapted as needed and applied in case of an urgent change. In such cases, Predişcan (2004) recommends a quick identification of the type of change that is needed, its implementation and then the author advises to return to the reducing resistance to change stage. Returning to this stage is imperative because if employees will not understand what, how and why it happened, they could sabotage the whole process and the change would be in vain.

In Lewin's, Moorhead – Griffin's, Beckhard – Harris's and Florescu – Popescu's Models, the reducing the resistance to change stage was not identified. These authors decided to omit this phase either because the employees participate in the change process and understand its necessity or because the employees do not oppose it.

In the other six models, respectively, Edgar Huse's, Rosabeth Moss Kanter's, John Kotter's, Tichy and Devanne's, and Nadler and Tushman's, the reducing resistance to change stage can be inferred through the methods, techniques, and procedures presented in different stages of the models.

The planning phase of Edgar Huse's Model assumes besides presenting the actions that need to be taken, that there is an identification of the employees' resistance to change. Although the model does not include a stage that is entitled "reducing resistance to change", the author stresses its importance from the planning phase. First, the author recommends the need to identify employees' resistance to change, secondly, to apply a series of measures to reduce it and only afterward, to implement the new change.

In Kanter's Model, the following three stages refer to reducing resistance to change:

- *Foster an environment of alliance:* the stage during which it is recommended to attract and involve all members in the process, and obtain their support in implementing the change;

- *Develop empowerment structures:* the stage during which employees are empowered. But before they are sent to training courses to gain the necessary skills to take over the new tasks. Kanter recommends that when employees are given certain tasks to accomplish, they should be rewarded accordingly. Providing resources, both financial and non-financial, is essential;

- *Communication, involvement and sincerity:* As means of reducing resistance to change, the author recommends open communication and employee involvement. People accept a change more rapidly when they are given all the information, know the advantages and disadvantages, and feel a part of the process.

Indirectly, Kanter also recommends first reducing resistance to change and only after obtaining the employees' support and involvement, to resort to the actual implementation.

Kotter makes a reference to the importance of reducing the resistance to change stage; his recommended methods being found in the following phases:

- *Creating a guiding coalition* stage which assumes attracting the key leaders of the change and encouraging the team members to work together. This stage refers to building a consensus.

- *Communicate the vision:* the author describing his model as "requiring many calls." An intensive communication is recommended due to the fact that the affected employees will get involved more actively in a change if they are contributing and know exactly what is happening. It is essential that the change agents communicate to the involved people why, where, how and when the change process will begin, and how it will affect them. Also, the employees must recognize that the transformation does not happen overnight and there will always be both gains and losses.

- *Empowering employees* presumes giving them the necessary authority to perform a task, as well as the needed knowledge and tools. It is believed that employees are less resistant if they have all the necessary information and are rewarded accordingly.

- *Short-term gains.* Any gain, however small it is, needs to be paid and communicated to the other members. Thus, people become more motivated to engage in the process because their involvement will be associated with a potential gain.

Constant communication and employees' accountability are two key ways to attract and engage staff in implementing a new change. People are excited to participate in something new when they know exactly what will happen, how they will be affected and what advantages will be received. As long as people feel that they have the necessary control and knowledge, the emergence of the resistance effect is not questioned.

As in the above-mentioned models, the reducing resistance to change stage, which can be drawn through the four shown stages, is located before the implementation stage. Kotter recommends that attracting and involving employees in the change process should be undertaken before the change is institutionalized.

A Reducing Resistance to Change Model

Analyzing several organizational change models, I've found that the reducing resistance to change stage is present, totally lacking, or it can be inferred. To successfully implement a new change, I consider that any manager or change agent must pay close attention to this stage. Of course, initially, a change can be implemented without the employees' support, but it does not mean that the new change will last. Being accustomed to a certain routine, people can always go back to their old habits, especially in those conditions when they do not perceive the necessity and importance of the new change. The role of the change agents is essential for the new change to become permanent. Change agents must communicate constantly with the employees, answering all their questions and when necessary, to involve the key members in the process.

Most methods of reducing this opposition to change originate from Kotter and Schlesinger's (1979) proposed six methods, resistance to change being generally considered as a negative phenomenon. Further, I propose a reducing resistance to change model (Figure 2), stressing that an effective manager must "use employees' resistance", in order to improve and refine the change process.

The proposed model is recommended when the manager or the change agent reaches the reducing resistance to change stage within an organizational change model. Depending on the position of the resistance to change stage, which is determined by the type of change that follows the implementation, the application of the model may occur before, during, or after the actual implementation of the change.

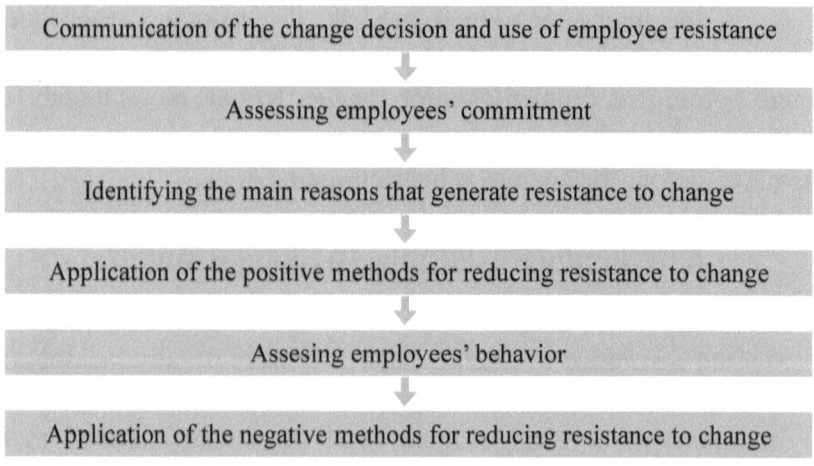

Figure 2: A reducing resistance to change model

1. Communication of the change decision and use of employee resistance

Communication of the change decision and use of employee resistance is the first phase of the model and requires an open communication between the change initiators and the affected members, so that the first would be able to announce openly the change decisions, and the last, to manifest their ideas regarding the changes in question.

Although many authors recommend communicating the change decision at a propitious time, the reality indicates that this is not always possible. In order to perceive more easily the new initiatives, I suggest the communication of the change decision in such a way that employees' would be able to openly express their views on the new process and have the opportunity to contribute with their own ideas. I emphasize the two-way communication, because often employees can provide great ideas which can be useful in improving the change process.

Manifestation of resistance to change from some employees is inevitable at this stage and so the change agent must use it to his or her advantage. Since the resistance phenomenon assumes certain strengths by using them the agent can gain the employees' support, diminishing their resistance. The most common way through which change agents respond to employees' reactions is "resisting their resistance, one force meeting the other" (Maurer, 1996). I believe that most often this approach is wrong, especially since the change agent can benefit from the use of their resistance (Ford et al., 2008, Ford and Ford, 2010). Furthermore, Fiorelli and Margolis (1993) state that a certain level of resistance may be beneficial for an organization.

In the present context, "the use of employee resistance" means hearing, considering, and implementing some ideas of those employees who are against change, because very often, the resistant people can provide valuable insights about how the proposed change may be amended in order to increase its chances of success. Employees who agree with the new change rarely will propose creative ideas to improve the process; these ideas being much more easily and quickly obtained from those who resist.

In case of a planned change, the change agent may reserve some time for talks with key employees and find out their views. The concern of the senior managers is to maintain or increase the organization's performance with all of the decisions being directed towards a positive end. There are multiple cases, however, where employees from the middle and lower levels, exercising their daily activities and facing certain problems, may perceive the new change from a different perspective. They may detect certain aspects that need remodeling, the result of which could have positive effects both on their work and the organization's performance.

I recommend for managers and change agents not to ignore the views of the employees who are opposed to change, but on the contrary, to use the valuable ones because sometimes the resistant employees can come up with creative ideas that will contribute to a more rapid and effective implementation of the change.

Furthermore, after communicating the change decision, finding out employees' views and considering the best of them, follows the second stage of the model.

2. Assessing employees' commitment

Assessing employees' commitment represents the second phase of the proposed model and involves analyzing the employees' degree of commitment towards the organization where they work.

Before deciding which reducing resistance to change methods must be applied, an effective change agent must assess the commitment of the members involved in the process and depending on the identified attitudes, propose a number of solutions. The change management consultant, Daryl Conner, says that "resistance and commitment are two sides of the same coin." Even if employees' resistance may not initially manifest, their lack of commitment could result in the appearance of a strong resistance to change throughout the process (Davidson, 2002: 23).

To achieve a full assessment it is recommended that the change agent analyze separately each type of organizational commitment, namely affective, continuous, and normative commitment, as each type has its own results and implications on the employees' behavior (Meyer and Allen, 1991).

Another important aspect that should not be overlooked is the need to assess the level of commitment in those circumstances when the organization's management wishes to retain the most talented professionals. If they are not sufficiently committed to the organization or satisfied with it, the management should take the necessary measures otherwise, the loss of the best specialists may have negative effects on the organization's performance. The organizations that face difficulties in retaining and replacing key employees will also encounter difficulties in optimizing the company's performance (Sarwar and Khalid, 2011: 671). As stated by the previously mentioned authors, in addition to the immediate recruitment costs, there will be other hidden costs related to time management and low productivity, as the new employees will require some time before becoming effective at the new tasks.

3. Identifying the main reasons that generate resistance to change

Simultaneously or immediately after assessing the employees' commitment, the change agent must identify the main reasons generating this reluctance to change, specific to each employee. This stage is very important because depending on the identified reason, a certain method for reducing resistance to change is proposed. Of course, the reasons for opposition will be different from one individual to another, depending on their own perception of the change process.

4. Application of the positive methods for reducing resistance to change

After assessing the employees' commitment and determining the main reasons that generate resistance, the change agent has already formed an opinion regarding the degree of resistance within the organization and can apply a series of positive methods to reduce it. I focus on applying the positive methods first because the change agent has to do his or her best to attract the affected members onto the side of change. Only after they understand the need for new implementations will they be willing to contribute to the process.

In order to effectively reduce the employees' resistance, I propose applying the following positive methods, with the condition that they will be applied in accordance with the identified reasons. The positive methods for reducing resistance to change are continuous communication, involvement, training, empowerment, financial and nonfinancial motivation, counseling and support and negotiation.

Each method has been described separately, the change agent assuming the task of choosing carefully the method or methods that respond better to the situation of the affected members and of course, to the organization's culture and management style.

5. Assessing employees' behavior

After applying the positive methods of reducing resistance to change, the change agent must evaluate the employees' new behavior. He or she must determine if the application of the methods had the desired effect and whether the support of the affected members was gained or not.

If there was success and resistance to change was diminished, the change agent can continue with the implementation of the new change. Otherwise, I emphasize the necessity of the completion of the sixth stage of the proposed model, namely, application of the negative methods for reducing resistance to change.

6. Application of the negative methods for reducing resistance to change

In order to effectively reduce employees' resistance, I first proposed to apply a set of positive methods but if they do not have the desired effect, the manager will have no alternative but to apply the negative methods of reducing resistance to change. Since implementing the new change represents a priority for the company, its management will not hesitate to apply the coercive methods where employees do not want to comply to the new procedures. They either adapt to new conditions or are penalized. It is believed that the management always has the organization's best interests in the mind (Predişcan, 2004) and if employees do not change their behavior in a timely manner or, if their values do not correspond with those of the organization, the management will have no alternative but to penalize them.

After conducting a study in the banking sector, I found that employees put more emphasis on their own interests than those of the organization (Braduțanu, 2012). It makes sense that an employee will cherish his every day routine and job security more than being exposed to some new changes that might cause potential disruptions. Here intervenes the role of the top managers who, as a priority, will put forth the organization's success and interests, and any incompatibility with these elements will be considered a negative factor that must be eliminated. For this reason, when the application of the positive methods fails or when the position of the change initiator towards the opposing members is very strong, the application of the negative methods represents the ideal solution.

References

1. Abu-Jarad, I., Yusof, N., Nikbin, D. (2010), *A Review Paper on Organizational Culture and Organizational Performance*, International Journal of Business and Social Science, 1(3), pp. 26-46.

2. Agboola A. A., Salawu R. O. (2011), *Managing Deviant Behavior and Resistance to Change*, International Journal of Business and Management, Vol. 6, No. 1, pp. 235-242.

3. Akbar, S., Yousaf, M., Haq, N., & Hunjra, A. (2011), *Impact of Employee Empowerment on Job Satisfaction: An Empirical Analysis of Pakistani Service Industry*, Interdisciplinary Journal of Contemporary Research in Business, 2(11), pp. 680-685.

4. Al-Ma'ani and A. Isma'il (2008), *Effect of Employees' Empowerment on the Realization of Distinction for Jordanian Institutions*, Participating in King Abdullah II's Prize for Distinction. Amman: Amman Arab University for Graduate Studies.

5. Arnetz B., Blomkvist, V. (2007). *Leadership, Mental Health, and Organizational Efficacy in Health Care Organizations*, Psychotherapy and Psychosomatics, 76, pp. 242-248.

6.   Beckhard R. (1969), *Organization Development: Strategies and Models,* Addison-Wesley, Reading, MA.

7.   Bennebroek Gravenhorst K. M. (2003), *A Different View on Resistance to Change.* Paper presented at the "Power Dynamics and Organizational Change IV" EAWOP Conference in Lisbon, Portugal, May 14-17, pp. 2-18.

8.   Brăduțanu Daniela (2011), *Identifying Motivational Factors within a Multinational Company,* ACTA UNIVERSITATIS DANUBIUS Vol. 7, No. 4, pp. 224-231.

9.   Brăduțanu Daniela (2012), *Identifying the Reducing Resistance to Change Phase in an Organizational Change Model,* ACTA UNIVERSITATIS DANUBIUS Vol. 8, No. 2, pp. 18-26.

10.   Brăduțanu Daniela (2012), *DO REALLY EMPLOYEES RESIST CHANGE? CASE STUDY AT A CREDIT INSTITUTION,* Proceedings of the Conference Challenges of the Knowledge Society, „Pro Universitaria" Bucharest, pp. 1263-1268.

11.   Brăduțanu Daniela (2013), *RESISTANCE TO CHANGE IN THE BANKING SECTOR: A COMPARISON BETWEEN ROMANIAN AND HUNGARIAN CREDIT INSTITUTIONS,* Applied Social Sciences: Economics and Politics, Cambridge Scholars Publishing, Vol. 1, pp. 19-28.

12.   Brown Michelle, Cregan Christina (2008), *Cynicism: The Role of Employee Involvement,* Human Resource Management, Vol. 47, No. 4, pp. 667–686.

13.   Burns T., Stalker G. M. (1961), *The Management of Innovation,* London: Tavistock.

14.   Caruth D., Middlebrook B., Rachel F. (1985), Overcoming Resistance to Change, Sam Advanced Management Journal, Copyright in 2001 by the Society for Advancement of Management.

15. Cercel M. (2012), *The Organizational Culture of Performant Companies,* Doctorate Thesis, Craiova, Romania.

16. Clark R., Hartline M., Jones K. (2009), *The Effects of Leadership Style on Hotel Employees' Commitment to Service Quality,* Cornell Hospitality Quarterly, 50(2), pp. 209.

17. Clarke Liz (2002), *Change Management,* Teora Publisher, Bucharest.

18. Cobb, A. T., Wooten, K. C. & Folger R. (1995), *Justice in the Making: Toward Understanding the Theory and Practice of Justice in Organizational Change and Development,* Research in Organizational Change and Development, pp. 243-295.

19. Czarniawska Barbara, Sevon G. (1996), *Translating Organizational Change,* Berlin: Walter de Gruyter.

20. Daft R. L. (2000), *Management,* Fifth edition, Fort Worth, PA

21. Davidson J. (2002), *Overcoming Resistance to Change,* Public Management, Vol. 84, Issue 11, pp. 20-23.

22. Dell Twyla (1988), *An Honest Day's Work. Motivating Employees to Give Their Best,* Crisp Pub Inc.

23. Dent E. B., Galloway Goldberg Susan (1999), *Challenging "Resistance to Change",* The Journal of Applied Behavioral Science, Vol. 35, No. 1, pp. 25-41.

24. Feldman M. S. (2004), *Resources in Emerging Structures and Processes of Change,* Organization Science, Vol. 15, pp. 295-309.

25. Fiorelli J. S., Margolis H. (1993), *Managing and Understanding Large System Change: Guidelines for Executives and Change Agents,* Organization Development Journal, Vol. 11, No. 3, pp. 1-13.

26. Folger R., Skarlicki D. P. (1999), *Unfairness and Resistance to Change: Hardship as Mistreatment,* Journal of Organizational Change Management, Vol. 12, No.1, pp. 35-50.

27. Forbes Farmer J. (2011), *The Effects of Staff Empowerment on Supervisory Relations, Burnout and Job Satisfaction: A Comparative Case Study of Two American Prisons,* International Journal of Business and Social Science, Vol. 2, No. 13, pp. 21-27.

28. Ford J. D., Ford Laurie W., D'Amelio A. (2008), *Resistance to Change: The Rest of the Story,* Academy of Management Review, Vol. 33, No. 2, pp. 362-377.

29. Ford J. D., Ford Laurie W. (2010), *Stop Blaming Resistance to Change and Start Using It,* Organizational Dynamics, Vol. 39, No. 1, pp. 24-36 .

30. Galle B., Leahy J. (2009), *Laboratories of Democracy? Policy Innovation in Decentralized Governments,* Emory Law Review, 58(6), pp. 1333-1400.

31. Gilley J. W. (2001), *The Manager as Change Agent: A Practical Guide to Developing High Performance, People and Organizations,* Basic Books.

32. Harvey T.R. (1995), *Checklist for Change: A Pragmatic Approach to Creating and Controlling Change.* Second edition. Lancaster PA: Technomic Publishing Inc.

33. Hennestad, B. (2002), *Implementing Participative Management: Transition Issues From the Field,* The Journal of Applied Behavioral Science, 36(3), 314-335.

34. Hultman K. (1998), *Making Change Irresistable: Overcoming Resistance to Change in Your Organization,* Davies – Black Publishing, Palo Alto, California.

35. Ispas Andreia Cristina (2012), *The Effects of the Leadership Study on Employees Individual Performance in the Hotel Industry, Doctorate Thesis,* West University of Timişoara, Romania.

36. Kanter Rosabeth Moss, Stein B. A., Jick Tood D. (1992), *The Challenge of Organizational Change-* Free Press, New York.

37. Kauffman C. (2010), *Employee Involvement: A New Blueprint for Success,* Journal of Accountancy, May, pp. 46-49.

38. Kee J. E., Newcomer K. E. (2008), *Why Do Change Efforts Fail,* Public Manager, Vol. 37, Issue 3, pp. 5-12.

39. Kotter, J., Schlesinger, L. (1979), *Choosing Strategies for Change,* Harvard Business Review, 57, pp. 106-114.

40. Kotter J. P. (1995), *Leading Change: Why Transformation Efforts Fail,* Harward Business Review, Vol. 57, No. 2, pp. 59-67.

41. Kumar S., Kant S., Amburgey T. L. (2007), *Public Agencies and Collaborative Management Approaches: Examining Resistance Among Administrative Professionals,* Administration and Society, Vol. 39, No. 5, pp. 569-611.

42. Larson G. S., Tompkins P. K. (2005), *Ambivalence and Resistance: A Study of Management in a Concertive Control System,* Communication Monographs.

43. Lawrence P. (1969), *How to Deal with Resistance to Change,* Harvard Business Review, Vol. 32, No. 3, pp. 49-57.

44. Lovallo D., Kahneman D. (2003), *Delusions of Success: How Optimism Undermines Executive Decisions,* Harvard Business Review, Vol. 81, No.7, pp. 56-63.

45. Luscher L. S., Lewis M. W. (2008), *Organizational Change and Managerial Sensemaking: Working Through Paradox,* Academy of Management Journal, Vol. 51, pp. 221-240.

46. Marquis B.L., Huston C.J. (2009), *Leadership Roles and Management Functions in Nursing: Theory and Application.* 6th edition. Philadelphia.

47. Maurer R. (1996), *Using Resistance to Build Support for Change*, Journal for Quality & Participation, June, pp. 56-63.

48. Meyer J. P., Allen N. J. (1991), *A Three Component Conceptualization of Organizational Commitment*, Human Resource Management Review, Vol.1, pp. 61-89.

49. Michelman P. (2007), *Overcoming Resistance to Change*, Harvard Management Update, 12, pp. 3-4.

50. Moorhead, G. Griffin R.(2009), *Organizational Behavior*, Ninth edition, Boston, Houghton Mifflin.

51. Muchinsky P.M. (2000), *Psychology Applied to Work*, London, Wadsworth.

52. Năstase M. (2004), *Organizational Culture* and Managerial Culture, ASE Publisher, Bucharest.

53. Năstase M. (2009), *Leadership in the Time of Change*, Review of International Comparative Management, Vol. 10, pp. 77-84.

54. Peccei R., Giangreco A., Sebastiano A. (2011), *The Role of Organizational Commitment in the Analysis of Resistance to Change*, Personnel Review, Vol. 40, No. 2, pp. 185-204.

55. Predișcan Mariana (2004), *Organizational Change: What, When and How to Change*, West University Publisher, Timișoara.

56. Predișcan Mariana, Săcui Violeta (2011), *Opportunity to Reduce Resistance to Change in a Process of Organizational Change*, Annals of the University of Oradea: Economic Science, Vol. 1, Issue 2, pp. 698-702.

57. Predişcan Mariana, Braduţanu Daniela (2012), *Change Agent – A Force Generating Resistance To Change Within An Organization?*, ACTA UNIVERSITATIS DANUBIUS, Vol. 8, No. 6, pp. 5-12.

58. Predişcan Mariana, Braduţanu Daniela, Roiban Roxana Nadina (2013), *Forces that Enhance or Reduce Employee Resistance to Change*, Annals of Faculty of Economics, Oradea, Vol. 1, Issue 1, pp. 1606-1612.

59. Sarwar A., Khalid Ayesha (2011), *Impact of Employee Empowerment on Employee's Job Satisfaction and Commitment with the Organization*, Interdisciplinary Journal of Contemporary Research in Business, Vol. 3, No. 2, pp. 664-683.

60. Siddique A., Khan M., Fatima U. (2011), *Impact of Academic Leadership on Faculty's Motivation and Organizational Effectiveness in Higher Education System*, International Journal of Business and Social Science, 2(8), pp. 184-191.

61. Smollan R. (2011), *Engaging with Resistance to Change*, University of Ackland Business Review, Vol. 13, No. 1, pp. 12-15.

62. Strebel, P. (1996). *Why Do Employees Resist Change*, Harvard Business Review, Vol. 74, No. 3, pp.86-92.

63. Tannenbaum R., Schmidt W. (1957), *How to Choose a Leadership Pattern*, Harvard Business Review, Vol. 51, May-June, pp. 162-180.

64. Thomas R., Hardy Cynthia (2011), *Reframing Resistance to Organizational Change*, Scandinavian Journal of Management, Vol. 27, pp. 322-331.

65. Thomas R., Linstead A. (2002), *Losing the Plot? Middle Managers and Identity*, Organization, Vol. 9, pp. 71-93.

66. Vasugi S.P., Manicka (2011). *An Emperical Investigation on Employee Empowerment Practices in Indian Software Industries*, International Journal of Contemporary Research in Business, 2(11), pp. 668-674.

67. Von Simson, E. M. (1990), *The Centrally Decentralized is Organization,* Harvard Business Review, 68, 158-161.

68. Waddell D., Sohal, A. S. (1998), *Resistance: A Constructive Tool for Change Management,* Management Decision, Vol. 36, No. 8, pp. 543-548.

69. Wagner J. A., Hollenbeck J. R. (2010), *Organizational Behavior. Securing Competitive Advantage,* Routledge, New York, pp. 283-293.

70. White G. (1998), *Planned Change*, In Rocchiccioli JT Tilbury MS (eds) *Clinical Leadership in Nursing,* Philadelphia, PA, WB Saunders Company.

71. Wooldridge B., Schmid T., Floyd S. W. (2008), *The Middle Management Perspective: Contributions, Synthesis and Future Research,* Journal of Management, Vol. 34, pp. 1190-1221.

72. Yao K., Cui X. (2010), *Study on the Moderating Effect of the Employee Psychological Empowerment on the Enterprise Employee Turnover Tendency: Taking Small and Middle Enterprises in Jinan as the Example,* International Business Research, 3(3), 21-31.

73. Zlate M. (2004), *Leadership and Management,* Iaşi: Polirom Publisher.

www.ingramcontent.com/pod-product-compliance
Lightning Source LLC
Chambersburg PA
CBHW021437170526

45164CB00001B/278